GOOGLE SHEETS MASTERY

FROM BEGINNER TO EXPERT IN ONE BOOK

ETHAN WELLS

Copyright © 2025 All rights reserved

The content contained within this book may not be reproduced, duplicated or transmitted without direct written permission from the author or the publisher.

Under no circumstances will any blame or legal responsibility be held against the publisher, or author, for any damages, reparation, or monetary loss due to the information contained within this book. Either directly or indirectly. You are responsible for your own choices, actions, and results.

Legal Notice:

This book is copyright protected. This book is only for personal use. You cannot amend, distribute, sell, use, quote or paraphrase any part, or the content within this book, without the consent of the author or publisher.

Disclaimer Notice:

By reading this document, the reader agrees that under no circumstances is the author responsible for any losses, direct or indirect, which are incurred as a result of the use of the information contained within this document, including, but not limited to, — errors, omissions, or inaccuracies.

TABLE OF CONTENTS

INTRODUCTION — 6

I. What This Book Will Teach You — 6
II. Who This Book Is For — 6
III. How to Use This Book — 7
IV. Why Google Sheets? — 7

CHAPTER 1: GETTING STARTED — 8

I. Welcome to Google Sheets — 8
II. Getting Access & Setting Up — 10
III. Navigating the Google Sheets Interface — 11
IV. Saving, Naming, and Sharing Your Sheet — 17
V. Quick Hands-On Project – Your First Sheet — 20
VI. Best Practices for Beginners — 21

CHAPTER 2: FORMATTING & ORGANIZING YOUR DATA — 23

I. Why Formatting and Organization Matter — 23
II. Formatting Text and Numbers — 24
III. Conditional Formatting Basics — 28
IV. Freezing Rows and Columns — 30
V. Sorting and Filtering Data — 32
VI. Data Validation and Drop-Down Lists — 35
VII. Hiding, Grouping & Protecting Data — 36
VIII. Practice Exercise – Organize This Sheet! — 38
IX. Tips and Best Practices — 39

CHAPTER 3: ESSENTIAL FORMULAS AND FUNCTIONS — 41

I. Introduction to Formulas — 41
II. Auto-Fill and Smart Formula Tools — 43

III.	Basic Math Functions Everyone Should Know	46
IV.	Understanding Formula Errors	49
V.	Tips for Beginners Using Formulas	52
VI.	Quick Challenges for Practice	54

CHAPTER 4: LOGICAL & LOOKUP FUNCTIONS 57

I.	Introduction to Logical Thinking in Sheets	57
II.	The IF Function (and Its Friends)	58
III.	Lookup Functions That Find Your Data	61
IV.	Advanced Lookup Tools	66
V.	Practical Scenarios and Projects	68

CHAPTER 5: TEXT, DATE, AND DATA FUNCTIONS 73

I.	Text Functions	73
II.	Date and Time Functions	76
III.	Data Transformation and Filtering Functions	80
IV.	Introduction to ARRAYFORMULA	83
V.	QUERY Function Essentials	86
VI.	Practice Projects	88
VII.	Tips and Best Practices	91

CHAPTER 6: CHARTS, GRAPHS & DASHBOARDS 96

I.	Why Visualization Matters	96
II.	Choosing the Right Chart	96
III.	Creating a Chart in Google Sheets	98
IV.	Advanced Chart Features	101
V.	Building an Interactive Dashboard	104
VI.	Using Slicers in Google Sheets	107
VII.	Linking Data Across Sheets for Dashboards	110
VIII.	Publishing and Sharing Dashboards	111

IX.	Practice Projects – Build Your Own Dashboards	113
X.	Tips for Better Visuals	118

CHAPTER 7: AUTOMATION WITH GOOGLE SHEETS — **120**

I.	Why Automate in Google Sheets?	120
II.	Introduction to Google Apps Script	121
III.	Automating Common Tasks	122
IV.	Creating Simple Custom Functions	124
V.	Connecting Sheets with IMPORT Functions	127
VI.	Google Forms + Sheets Integration	130
VII.	Connecting to Other Google Services	133
VIII.	Best Practices for Sheet Automation	135
IX.	Mini Automation Projects	137

CHAPTER 8: PRODUCTIVITY TIPS, SHORTCUTS & ADVANCED TROUBLESHOOTING — **140**

I.	Keyboard Shortcuts That Speed Everything Up	140
II.	Collaboration Tips for Teams	141
III.	Optimizing Performance in Large Sheets	143
IV.	Pro-Level Tips & Hidden Features	144
V.	End-of-Chapter Checklist	145

CONCLUSION & BONUSES — **147**

I.	Google Sheets Mastery: From Beginner to Expert in One Book	147
II.	Keep the Momentum Going	147

THANK YOU — **149**

INTRODUCTION

Google Sheets has become much more than just a free spreadsheet alternative. It's a powerful, cloud-based tool used by students, teachers, entrepreneurs, analysts, and Fortune 500 companies alike. From tracking personal budgets and running businesses to automating tasks and visualizing data, Google Sheets can do it all - if you know how.

Whether you're a complete beginner staring at your first blank spreadsheet or a self-taught user looking to finally master formulas, automation, and dashboards - this book is your all-in-one guide to unlocking the full potential of Google Sheets.

I. WHAT THIS BOOK WILL TEACH YOU

In plain, practical language, this book will walk you through everything you need to know, including:

- Navigating Google Sheets like a pro - even if you've never used it.
- Organizing and formatting your data for clarity and efficiency.
- Mastering essential and advanced formulas (like IF, VLOOKUP, QUERY, and ARRAYFORMULA).
- Creating interactive dashboards and dynamic charts.
- Automating your workflows with Google Apps Script.
- Integrating Google Sheets with other tools like Forms, Calendar, Gmail, and more.
- Building real-world templates you can actually use - budget trackers, CRMs, invoice generators, and more.

You won't just learn what each feature does - you'll learn how to apply it in practical, real-world scenarios.

II. WHO THIS BOOK IS FOR

This book is designed for:

- Beginners who want a no-jargon, hands-on approach.
- Busy professionals looking to automate repetitive tasks.
- Students and educators who want smarter ways to manage class data and assignments.
- Entrepreneurs and freelancers building lean, powerful systems

- without expensive software.
- Anyone who's ever thought, "There's got to be an easier way to do this in Sheets".

No prior experience is required. All you need is a Google account and the willingness to click around and experiment.

III. HOW TO USE THIS BOOK

The chapters are arranged in a progressive flow - from the basics to advanced skills - so you can either read it straight through or skip to the sections you need most.

- Practice along with downloadable templates.
- Try mini-projects at the end of key chapters.
- Access free bonus resources, cheat sheets, and walkthroughs (details inside).

This book is meant to be interactive and practical. You won't just read - you'll do.

IV. WHY GOOGLE SHEETS?

Because it's free. It's fast. It's flexible. And because knowing how to use Google Sheets gives you a competitive edge in school, in work, and in business.

By the end of this book, you'll be able to build tools, solve problems, and automate your workflows using the same spreadsheet software trusted by millions around the world.

Ready to go from beginner to expert?

Let's get started.

CHAPTER 1: GETTING STARTED

I. WELCOME TO GOOGLE SHEETS

1. WHAT IS GOOGLE SHEETS?

Google Sheets is a cloud-based spreadsheet application developed by Google. Think of it as the modern-day spreadsheet tool that lives entirely online and allows you to work, collaborate, and automate from anywhere in the world - with no need to install any software.

It's part of the Google Workspace suite (formerly known as G Suite), which includes tools like Google Docs, Google Slides, Google Forms, Gmail, Calendar, and Drive. If you have a Google account, you already have access to Google Sheets - for free.

Let's look at what makes Google Sheets so powerful:

- Cloud-Based & Always Up-to-Date: Your files are saved in the cloud in real time - no more hitting "Save" every 5 minutes.
- Access from Any Device: Whether you're on a laptop, smartphone, tablet, or just borrowing a friend's computer, your spreadsheets are one login away.
- No Software Installation Required: No need for CD installs or hefty Excel licenses. Just open your browser and start working.
- Works with or without the Internet: To turn on offline mode, go to File → Make available offline. Once it's on, you can open and edit Sheets without internet, and changes will sync when you reconnect.
- Integrated with Other Google Tools: Easily link Sheets with Forms, Gmail, Calendar, and even Google Analytics for powerful workflows.

2. WHY USE GOOGLE SHEETS OVER EXCEL?

While Excel has long been the spreadsheet standard, Google Sheets offers several advantages—especially in today's connected, cloud-based world. Here's a quick breakdown:

Feature	Google Sheets	Microsoft Excel
Cost	Free with a Google account	Requires purchase or Office 365 subscription
Access	Web-based + mobile app	Desktop + Office online (limited features)

Feature	Google Sheets	Microsoft Excel
Real-Time Collaboration	☑ Built-in and seamless	☑ Requires OneDrive or SharePoint
Autosave	☑ Automatic in real time	✗ Needs manual or OneDrive sync
Cloud Integration	Native with Google Drive	Microsoft OneDrive or third-party
Add-ons & Automation	Google Apps Script, Add-ons store	VBA, Power Query, Power Automate
Best For	Collaboration, sharing, automation	Advanced modeling, macros, power analysis

While Excel remains the powerhouse for complex, enterprise-level analysis, Google Sheets is often the faster, lighter, and more collaborative solution - especially for small businesses, students, freelancers, and teams.

3. REAL-LIFE USE CASES

Still not sure if Sheets fits into your life or business? Here are some practical, everyday examples where Google Sheets shines:

- Personal Use:
  - » Monthly budgeting or expense tracking.
  - » Meal planning and grocery lists.
  - » Habit or workout trackers.
  - » Vacation itinerary planner.
- Academic Use:
  - » Gradebooks and attendance sheets.
  - » Class schedules and assignment deadlines.
  - » Project group collaboration.
  - » Research data collection and analysis.
- Business Use:
  - » Employee schedules and time tracking.
  - » Sales dashboards and revenue reports.
  - » CRM (Customer Relationship Management).
  - » Project timelines and Kanban boards.
  - » Inventory management.

- Freelancer Use:
  » Client proposal and contract templates.
  » Time logs for hourly billing.
  » Invoice generation and tracking.
  » Social media content calendars.

Whether you're managing your household expenses, tracking inventory for a small business, or collaborating with your team remotely, Google Sheets can be molded to fit just about any workflow.

II. GETTING ACCESS & SETTING UP

1. CREATING A GOOGLE ACCOUNT (SKIP IF ALREADY HAVE ONE)

To use Google Sheets, you need a Google Account - which is free and takes less than 2 minutes to create.

If you already use Gmail, YouTube, or Google Drive, you're good to go. But if not, follow these simple steps:

1. Go to https://accounts.google.com/signup.
2. Enter your **first and last name.**
3. Choose a **username** (this becomes your Gmail address).
4. Set a **password** and confirm it.
5. Click **Next** and follow the verification steps.

Once your account is ready, you can access all Google tools—including Sheets, Docs, Slides, Forms, and Drive.

2. ACCESSING GOOGLE SHEETS

There are multiple ways to open Google Sheets depending on your workflow. Here are the most popular options:

Option 1: Direct URL

Go to https://sheets.google.com. This takes you straight to your Sheets dashboard where you can start a new file or open a recent one.

Option 2: Google Drive

1. Visit https://drive.google.com.
2. Click the **"+ New"** button on the left, then select **Google Sheets.**

This is especially helpful if you want to keep your spreadsheets organized.

Option 3: The Google Apps Launcher ("Waffle" Icon)

1. While in Gmail or any Google app, look for the 3×3 grid icon (top-right corner).
2. Click it to open the app menu.
3. Select **Sheets** from the list.

3. STARTING A NEW SPREADSHEET

Once you're inside Google Sheets, you'll see two main options at the top:

- Blank Spreadsheet – An empty canvas to start fresh.
- Template Gallery – A treasure trove of ready-to-use spreadsheets.

Tip: Templates are great for getting started fast. You'll find templates for:

- To-do lists.
- Calendars.
- Monthly budgets.
- Expense trackers.
- Invoices.
- Attendance sheets.

You can use these as-is or customize them for your specific needs.

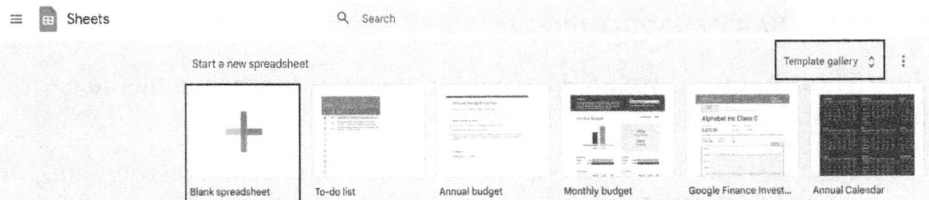

III. NAVIGATING THE GOOGLE SHEETS INTERFACE

Before you dive into formulas, formatting, and automation, it's important to feel comfortable with the layout of Google Sheets. Once you know where everything is, you'll work faster and more confidently.

1. LAYOUT OVERVIEW

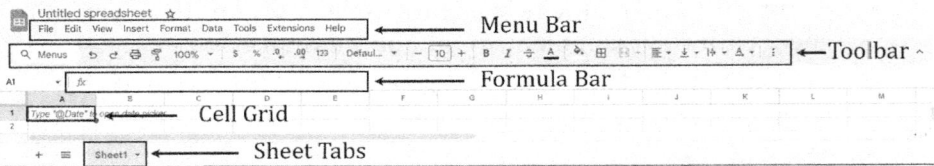

11

When you open a new Google Sheet, here's what you'll see:

Component	Description
Menu Bar	Located at the very top (File, Edit, View, Insert, Format, etc.). This is where you'll find most features like printing, sharing, and advanced tools.
Toolbar	Just below the menu bar, this contains quick-access buttons for font styles, fill colors, text alignment, borders, and more.
Formula Bar	Located below the toolbar. This is where you enter or edit formulas and see the contents of the selected cell.
Cell Grid	The main body of the spreadsheet—organized into columns (labeled A, B, C…) and rows (labeled 1, 2, 3…). Each square is a cell (e.g., A1, B2).
Sheet Tabs	At the bottom, you can see and manage multiple sheets in one file. Think of these like tabs in a notebook.
Quick Summary Bar	Shows sum, average, min, max of selected cells

In 2025–2026, Google updated the toolbar with cleaner icons, a new quick-formatting panel, and an improved summary bar that shows real-time totals when you highlight cells.

The Menu Bar in Google Sheets:

File: Think of this as your "office admin" menu — for managing the entire document.

- New / Open / Make a copy: Start a new file, open existing ones, or clone the current one.
- Import: Add data from Excel files, CSV, TSV, or another Google Sheet.
- Download: Export to Excel (.xlsx), PDF, .csv, and other formats.
- Email: Email the spreadsheet or as an attachment.
- Version History: See all changes made and restore previous versions.
- Share:
  » Share with Others: Invite specific people or groups to access your sheet with view, comment, or edit permissions.
  » Publish to Web: Make a live, publicly accessible version of your sheet that anyone can view online.
- Move to Trash: Deletes the file.

- Make Available Offline: Access and edit your spreadsheet even without an internet connection.
- Security Limitations: Some features or add-ons may be restricted based on your account's security settings.
- Print: Generate a clean, formatted version of your sheet for paper or PDF output.

EDIT: Handles changes to cell content and structure.

- Undo / Redo: Step backward or forward.
- Cut / Copy / Paste: Standard clipboard functions.
- Paste Special: Paste only values, formatting, or formulas.
- Find and Replace: Search and replace across the entire sheet.
- Delete Row/Column: Removes selected rows or columns, notes.

VIEW: Controls what you see and how it's displayed.

- Show: Display or hide selected elements in your sheet.
  - » Formula Bar: Show or hide the formula entry field.
  - » Gridlines: Show/hide the sheet's cell borders.
  - » Formulas: Display the actual formulas in cells instead of their calculated results.
  - » Protect Ranges: View areas locked from editing..
- Freeze: Lock specific rows or columns in place so they stay visible while you scroll.
- Group: Collapse or expand selected rows or columns to organize large datasets more easily.
- Comment: Toggle the display of comments and discussion threads directly on your sheet
- Zoom: Resize your sheet visually.
- Full screen: Hide menus for distraction-free working.

INSERT: Everything you might want to add into your spreadsheet.

- Rows, columns, cells, and sheets: Insert structure.
- Prebuilt Table: Quickly insert a professionally formatted table to organize data instantly.
- Charts: Add visual graphs based on your data.
- Pivot Table: Generate a dynamic summary table to analyze and explore large datasets efficiently.

- Images / Drawings: Add logos, icons, or custom graphics.
- Functions: Insert built-in formulas like SUM, IF, etc.
- Links: Add hyperlinks to websites or other sheets.
- Checkboxes: Add clickable checkboxes (for task lists, forms, etc.)
- Dropdown: Insert a selectable list of predefined options into a cell.
- Emoji: Add emojis directly into cells to visually highlight or categorize information.
- Smart Chips: Insert interactive chips that display enriched info such as people, dates, files, or links.
- Note / comment: Add annotations or collaborate.

FORMAT: Where you beautify your sheet.

- Theme: Apply a cohesive color and style scheme to your entire sheet.
- Number formats: Currency, percent, dates, etc.
- Text styles: Bold, italic, underline, font size/color.
- Alignment: Left, center, right, vertical alignments.
- Text wrapping: Wrap, clip, or overflow long text.
- Rotation: Adjust the angle of text within cells for clearer layout or emphasis.
- Smart Chips: Format smart chips to refine how people, dates, and other chip types appear in your sheet.
- Font Size: Change the size of the text in selected cells for readability or emphasis.
- Conditional formatting: Automatically style cells based on values.
- Alternating colors: Add zebra-striping for easier reading.
- Clear Formatting: Remove all formatting and return cells to the default style.

DATA: Manage and manipulate your actual data.

- Sort range / sheet: Sort by column A to Z or Z to A.
- Create a filter: Add filter buttons to column headers.
- Create Group by View: Group rows or columns dynamically based on specific criteria for easier data analysis.
- Create Filter View: Apply filters to view or analyze data without affecting what others see.
- Add a Slicer: Insert an interactive filter control to quickly filter pivot

tables or ranges.
- Protect Sheets and Ranges: Restrict editing access to specific cells, ranges, or entire sheets.
- Named ranges: Assign a name to a cell range.
- Named Functions: Create custom functions with names for reuse across your spreadsheet.
- Column Stats: Quickly see summary statistics, distributions, and visualizations for a selected column.
- Data validation: Add rules (like drop-downs or number limits).
- Data Cleanup: Quickly find and fix inconsistencies, duplicates, or formatting issues in your spreadsheet.
- Split Text to Column: Separate text in a cell into multiple columns based on a delimiter.
- Data Extraction: Extract structured information from unstructured data using formulas or AI.
- Data Connectors: Link your sheet to external data sources to import and refresh data automatically.

TOOLS: Where you find the "smart" and automation features.
- Create a New Form: Generate a Google Form linked to your sheet to collect responses directly.
- Spelling: Spell check your entries.
- Suggestion Controls: Manage how collaborators can suggest edits instead of making direct changes.
- Notification Settings: Set alerts to be notified when changes occur in your spreadsheet.
- Accessibility: Enable features and tools to make your spreadsheet easier to use for all users.

EXTENSIONS: Third-party tools and scripts live here.
- Add-ons: Install and manage external apps.
- Macros: Record and reuse actions across sheets.
- Apps Script: Jump straight into scripting for automation.
- AppSheet: Build custom apps directly from your spreadsheet without coding.
- Looker Studio: Create interactive dashboards and reports using your sheet's data.
- QR Code Generator: Generate QR codes from cell values to easily share links or information.

HELP: Find documentation and answers.

- Search the Menus: Quickly find commands and options across all menus in your spreadsheet.
- Sheets Help: Access Google Sheets documentation and guides for assistance.
- Help Sheets Improve: Provide feedback to Google to help enhance Sheets features.
- Privacy Policy: View Google's policies regarding data collection and privacy.
- Terms of Service: Review the rules and conditions for using Google Sheets.
- Function List: Browse all available formulas and functions with descriptions and usage examples.
- Keyboard Shortcuts: Opens the full shortcut list.

2. UNDERSTANDING SMART CHIPS

Google Sheets now supports "smart chips," interactive elements you can insert directly into a cell.

Find them through:

Insert → Smart chip

Types of chips:

- People chip: Assign a name from your contacts to easily track and collaborate with others.
- File chip: Link directly to Google Drive files for quick access.
- Calendar event chip: Display a preview of an event from Google Calendar.
- Place chip: Insert a Google Maps location for clear, visual references.
- Finance chip: Pull real-time financial data such as stock prices or exchange rates.
- Rating chip: Add ratings or score indicators to visualize levels or preferences.

Smart chips make sheets easier to read and automate, and they're now standard in Google templates.

3. UNDERSTANDING CELLS, ROWS, AND COLUMNS

Here's a quick refresher on spreadsheet basics:

- Columns: Run vertically and are labeled with letters (A, B, C, etc.).
- Rows: Run horizontally and are labeled with numbers (1, 2, 3, ...).
- Cells: The intersection of a row and column, identified by their cell address, such as A1 for Column A, Row 1, C5 for Column C, Row 5. Each cell can hold data like:
  » Text (e.g., "Groceries").
  » Numbers (e.g., 25.00).
  » Formulas (e.g., =A1+B1).
  » Dates, checkboxes, dropdowns, chips. links, and more.

4. ENTERING DATA FOR THE FIRST TIME

Try this to get a feel for it:

1. Click on cell A1 and type: Apples.
2. Hit Tab to move to cell B1 and type: 4.
3. Hit Enter to move to the cell directly below (B2).

You've now made your first data entry!

Editing or Deleting:

- Double-click a cell to edit its contents.
- Or, click once and use the formula bar at the top.
- To delete: press the Delete or Backspace key.

Try a Simple Formula:

1. Click on cell B2.
2. Type =2+2 and hit Enter.
3. The result will appear instantly as **4** - your first formula!

IV. SAVING, NAMING, AND SHARING YOUR SHEET

Google Sheets was built with real-time collaboration in mind. Unlike traditional spreadsheets, you don't have to worry about saving constantly or wondering who has the latest version - it's all handled seamlessly in the background. Let's break down how it works.

1. NAMING YOUR SPREADSHEET

By default, every new Google Sheet is titled "Untitled spreadsheet." Here's how to give it a proper name:

1. Click on "Untitled spreadsheet" at the top-left of your screen.
2. Type a new name like "Monthly Budget - April" or "Team Task List".
3. Press Enter to save the new name.

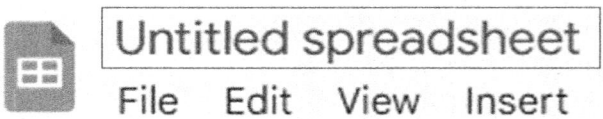

Tip: Use clear, searchable names so you can easily find your files later in Google Drive. Add dates or categories to help organize things.

2. Automatic Saving & Version History

Google Sheets autosaves your work in real time - literally every few keystrokes. There's no "Save" button because it's constantly saving for you.

But what if you want to go back to an earlier version? Here's how:

1. Go to the File menu.
2. Select Version history > See version history.
3. On the right side, you'll see a list of all saved versions, sorted by date and time.
4. Click any version to preview and restore it.

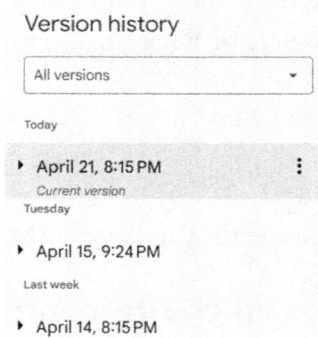

You can even name specific versions for milestones like "Initial Draft" or "Final Submission."

3. Sharing & Permissions

This is where Google Sheets really shines. You can share your sheet with others and collaborate in real time.

To Share Your Spreadsheet:

1. Click the blue **"Share"** button in the top-right corner.
2. In the pop-up window, you can enter specific email addresses or click "Copy link" to share with a group.

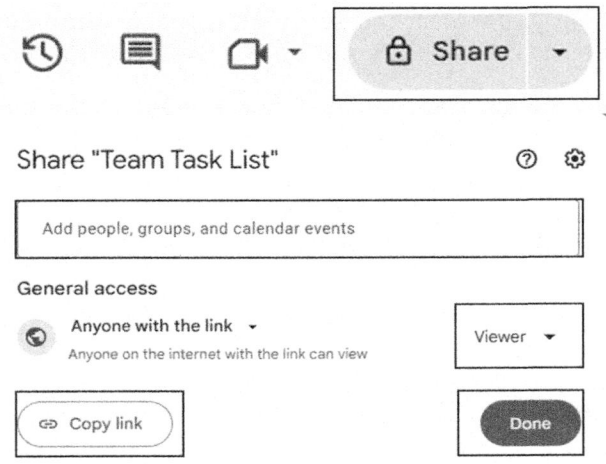

Set Permissions:

You can control how others interact with your spreadsheet:

Permission	What They Can Do
Viewer	Only view the content—can't edit or comment
Commenter	Leave comments, but can't change the content
Editor	Full editing access, including formatting, formulas, and structure

Collaborator Presence:

- When others are editing the sheet at the same time, you'll see their colored avatar icons in the top-right corner.
- Changes appear in real time, with different users highlighted by color.
- Use the chat feature (if available) to communicate directly.

Comments and Notes:

- Comments are great for team discussions or review notes:
    » Right-click a cell → Comment. You can tag people using @email.
- Notes are like sticky notes for your own reference: Right-click a cell → Insert note.

Notes remain private to the creator, while comments are shared with other collaborators and now support task assignment.

V. QUICK HANDS-ON PROJECT – YOUR FIRST SHEET

Let's put everything you've learned so far into practice by building two simple spreadsheets: a Grocery List and a Basic Expense Tracker.

These beginner-friendly projects will give you immediate confidence using cells, formatting, and simple functions.

1. CREATING A SIMPLE GROCERY LIST

This list will help you keep track of what you need to buy—and which items you've already picked up.

Step-by-Step Setup:

1. Open a new blank Google Sheet. In **cell A1**, type Item, in **cell B1**, type Quantity, in **cell C1**, type Bought.
2. Next, enter a few example items starting in row 2.
3. Add Checkboxes to track what you've bought:

» Select cells **C2 to C4.**

» Go to **Insert > Checkbox.** Now you can check off items as you shop!

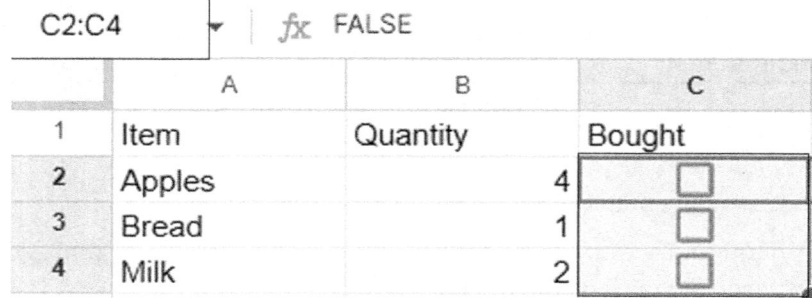

2. CREATING A BASIC EXPENSE TRACKER

This project helps you monitor spending and get familiar with typing data and using basic math functions.

Step-by-Step Setup:

1. In a new sheet, enter these headers in row 1:

	A	B	C	D
1	Date	Item	Category	Amount

2. Add sample data starting from row 2:

	A	B	C	D
1	Date	Item	Category	Amount
2	04/01/2025	Coffee	Food	4.5
3	04/02/2025	Gasoline	Travel	30
4	04/03/2025	Book	Education	12.99

Format the Amount Column:

3. Select column D.
4. Go to Format > Number > Currency. Your numbers should now show with a dollar sign (or your local currency).

Calculate Total Spending:

5. In the next empty row below your data, type Total: in column C.
6. In column D of that row, enter this formula: =SUM(D2:D4). This adds up all your listed expenses.

D5 *fx* =SUM(D2:D4)

	A	B	C	D
1	Date	Item	Category	Amount
2	04/01/2025	Coffee	Food	$4.50
3	04/02/2025	Gasoline	Travel	$30.00
4	04/03/2025	Book	Education	$12.99
5			Total	$47.49

VI. BEST PRACTICES FOR BEGINNERS

Creating your first few spreadsheets is exciting—but the real magic happens when you start building habits that make your work cleaner, faster, and easier to manage.

1. KEEP THINGS ORGANIZED

A well-organized sheet is easier to understand, share, and maintain.

- Name Your Files Clearly: Avoid vague names like "Sheet1" or "Test." Use descriptive titles like: Q2_Sales_Report_2025.
- Name Your Tabs: Rename sheet tabs (bottom left) by double-clicking them. For example: Summary, Data Entry, Expenses, or Week 1.
- Use Google Drive Folders: Group related spreadsheets together in folders. Color-code folders in Drive for quick visual reference.
- Color-Code Tabs for Clarity: Right-click a tab > Change color. This is helpful when working with multiple sheets in one file.

2. AVOID COMMON MISTAKES

It's easy to make small missteps that lead to confusion or incorrect results. Here's how to dodge them early on:

- Overwriting Formulas:
  » Always double-check before typing over a formula cell.
  » Use protected ranges for critical formulas when sharing.
- Forgetting to Use Cell References:
  » Instead of typing =4+5+6, use =A1+B1+C1 so your results update when values change.
- Inconsistent Formatting:
  » Use consistent currency/date formats throughout.
  » Highlight headers and total rows to avoid confusion.

3. TIPS FOR SMOOTH WORKFLOW

- Pin Important Files in Google Drive: Right-click a file > Add to Starred. This gives you fast access your important sheets.
- Bookmark Google Sheets: Bookmark https://sheets.google.com for fast access to recent files.
- Use Version History Regularly: Before making major changes, name the current version: File > Version history > Name current version.
- Get Comfortable with Undo: Press Ctrl + Z (Windows) or Cmd + Z (Mac) to undo any mistake instantly.

By applying these habits early, you'll save yourself time, headaches, and cleanup later on.

CHAPTER 2: FORMATTING & ORGANIZING YOUR DATA

I. WHY FORMATTING AND ORGANIZATION MATTER

1. THE ROLE OF GOOD FORMATTING

Google Sheets is more than just rows and columns—it's a data canvas, and how you format your spreadsheet directly impacts how effectively it communicates.

Here's why formatting matters:

- Clarity: Well-formatted sheets are easy to read and understand at a glance.
- Professionalism: Clean design impresses clients, teachers, coworkers, and anyone you share your work with.
- Functionality: Good formatting improves usability. It helps users navigate sheets faster, make fewer errors, and interpret data correctly.
- Error Reduction: A tidy layout makes mistakes easier to spot—whether it's a wrong formula, a missing entry, or duplicated information.

2. EXAMPLES OF POOR VS EXCELLENT FORMATTING

Let's compare two versions of the same data:

Poor Formatting:

	A	B	C
1	Groceries	Apples	3
2		Milk	1
3		bread	
4		Cheese	2

» Inconsistent capitalization.
» Missing values.
» No borders or headers.
» Uneven alignment.
» Hard to scan or understand.

Excellent Formatting:

	A	B	C
1	**Category**	**Item**	**Quantity**
2	Groceries	Apples	3
3	Groceries	Milk	1
4	Groceries	Bread	1
5	Groceries	Cheese	2

» Capitalized and consistent text.
» Headers are bold and centered.
» Numbers are right-aligned.
» Borders separate data from headers.
» No empty cells.

Good formatting turns raw data into information people can actually use. It's the difference between a spreadsheet that looks like homework... and one that looks like a report ready for your boss or client.

II. FORMATTING TEXT AND NUMBERS

Formatting doesn't just make your sheet look nice—it makes it easier to read, interpret, and use. In this section, we'll walk through how to adjust fonts, colors, alignment, and number formats so your spreadsheet not only works well but looks polished too.

1. CHANGING FONT STYLE, SIZE, AND COLOR

How to Format Text:

1. Select a cell or range of cells.
2. Use the toolbar at the top:
   » Font dropdown – Choose a style (e.g., Arial, Verdana).
   » Font size – Pick a size (usually 10–12 for body text, 14+ for headers).
   » Bold, Italic, Underline – Click icons or use shortcuts: Ctrl + B = Bold, Ctrl + I = Italic, Ctrl + U = Underline.

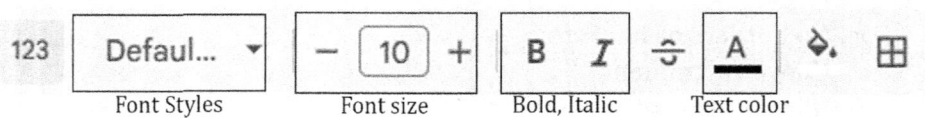

24

Pro Tips:

- Use bold for headers.
- Stick to 1–2 fonts throughout a sheet.
- Use text color sparingly for emphasis (e.g., red for warnings).

2. ALIGNING AND WRAPPING TEXT

Alignment is key to readability—especially in tables with mixed data types.

Alignment Options:

- Horizontal: Left, Center, Right.
- Vertical: Top, Middle, Bottom.
- Available in the toolbar via the alignment icons.

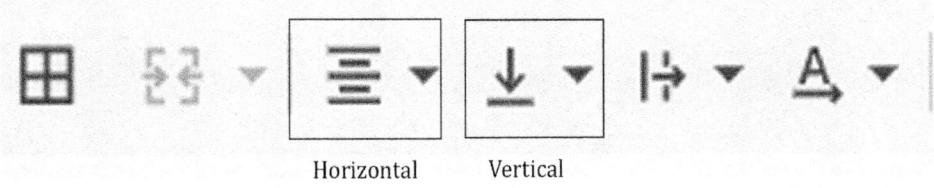

Horizontal   Vertical

Text Wrapping:

Sometimes, text overflows beyond a cell's border. You can wrap it to make everything visible without stretching the column too wide.

Clipped text   Wrapped text

To enable wrapping:

1. Select the cell(s).
2. Click Format > Wrapping > Wrap.

3. CELL FILL COLORS AND BORDERS

Using background colors and borders helps structure your sheet and draw attention to key areas.

Fill Color:

- Select cells > Click the paint bucket icon in the toolbar.
- Use light shades for headers or totals. Avoid overly bright or dark colors that make text hard to read.

Borders:

- Select cells > Click the borders icon.
- Choose styles: all borders, outer border, inner lines, thick line. Borders help define tables and separate sections.

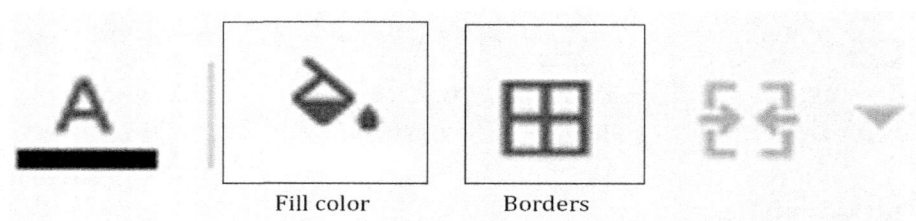

Fill color   Borders

Best Practice:

- Use borders + bold headers + light fill = clean, easy-to-read table.

	A	B	C
1	**Parent Task**	**Subtask**	**Status**
2	Project X	Plan the project	In Progress
3	Project X	Gather materials	Completed
4	Project X	Assign tasks	In Progress
5	Project X	Prepare report	In Progress
6	Project Y	Design interface	Completed
7	Project Y	Develop features	In Progress

4. NUMBER FORMATTING OPTIONS

Google Sheets lets you format numbers based on the type of data—currency, percent, decimal, and more.

To access number formatting:

1. Select a cell or range.
2. Go to Format > Number.
3. Choose from options like:
   » Number – Adds commas (e.g., 1,000).
   » Currency – Adds your local symbol (e.g., $1,000.00).
   » Percent – Converts decimals into percentages (e.g., 0.85 → 85%).
   » Plain Text – Keeps the number exactly as typed (no formatting).

Tip: You can also use Custom number formats if you want to create your own style (we'll explore this in later chapters).

5. DATE AND TIME FORMATTING

Dates can appear in many styles. Choose one that fits your audience and project.

Entering Dates: Google Sheets will automatically recognize common formats like: 4/6/2025 or April 6, 2025.

Changing the Display Format:

1. Select date cells.
2. Go to Format > Number > Date.
3. Or choose More formats > Custom date and time for styles like:
   » 6-Apr-25
   » April 6, 2025
   » 2025-04-06

6. SMART FILL AND SMART CLEANUP

Google Sheets now comes with improved smart assistance features that help clean and organize your data automatically.

Smart Fill appears as you type and can:

- Suggest patterns based on your data.
- Auto-complete entries.
- Build formulas automatically.

- Detect when text should be split into separate columns.

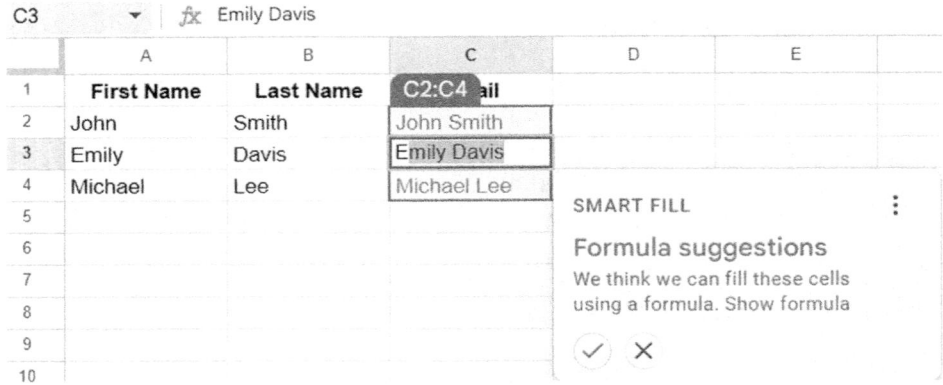

Smart Cleanup helps you fix:

- Identify and highlight duplicate entries.
- Fix inconsistent formatting automatically.
- Suggest cleanup actions when your sheet needs organizing.

These features appear automatically as suggestions in the bottom-right corner of your sheet.

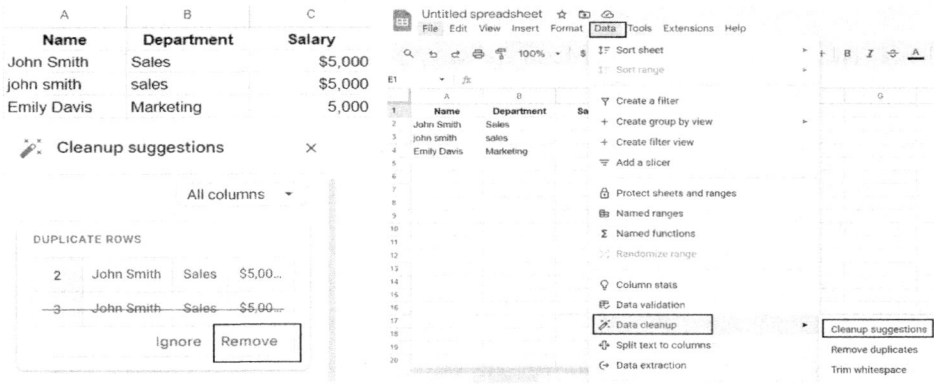

III. CONDITIONAL FORMATTING BASICS

1. WHAT IS CONDITIONAL FORMATTING?

Conditional formatting lets you change the appearance of cells automatically—based on their content. You can highlight values that meet certain conditions, color-code categories, or even visualize trends (like high and low values). Conditional formatting is widely used to:

- Instantly spot outliers or trends.
- Make reports and dashboards more visual.
- Create rules that update dynamically as data changes.
- Works great with checklists, score sheets, budgets, gradebooks, etc.

2. APPLYING CONDITIONAL FORMATTING

Let's walk through an example: Highlighting expenses over $300.

	A	B	C	D	E
1	Category	Item	Quantity	Unit price	Cost
2	Products	Digital Drawing Tablet	1	$350.00	$350.00
3	Products	Headphones	1	$110.00	$110.00
4	Products	Laptop	1	$1,100.00	$1,100.00
5	Products	Mouse	1	$35.00	$35.00
6	Products	Notebooks	3	$10.00	$30.00
7	Products	Pens	3	$2.00	$6.00
8	Products	Printer	1	$250.00	$250.00
9	Products	Printer paper	1	$10.00	$10.00

Step-by-Step:

1. Select the range of cells you want to format (E2:E9 or column E).
2. Go to Format > Conditional formatting or right-click > Conditional formatting.
3. A sidebar will appear on the right.
4. Under Format cells if..., choose Greater than. Enter a value (300).
5. Choose a format style (e.g., bold red text or light red background).
6. Click Done.

That's it! Now every value over 300 will be highlighted automatically.

Common Rule Examples:

- Color-code categories: Assign different colors for each item in a dropdown (e.g., Project Status).
- Highlight blanks or errors: Use "Is empty" or "Text contains" to flag missing data.
- Overdue dates: Compare with =TODAY() to find dates that have passed.

- Grade thresholds: Highlight scores below 60 in red, 60–80 in yellow, 80+ in green.

3. EDITING AND REMOVING RULES

As your data grows, you may need to update or delete formatting rules.

To Edit:
1. Click any cell in the formatted range.
2. Go to Format > Conditional formatting.
3. In the sidebar, click on the rule you want to change.
4. Adjust the condition, range, or formatting style.

To Remove:
1. Click on the rule.
2. Hit the trash bin icon to delete it.

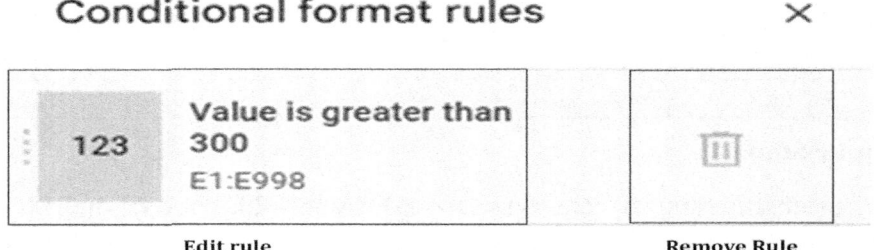

Edit rule   Remove Rule

Tips:
- Use multiple rules for color gradients (e.g., red → yellow → green).
- Pair with drop-down lists to highlight status-based items.
- Conditional formatting updates in real time as your data changes.

IV. FREEZING ROWS AND COLUMNS

1. WHY FREEZE ROWS/COLUMNS?

When you're scrolling through a long list of data—like sales records, gradebooks, or inventory logs—it's easy to lose track of what each column or row represents.

That's where freezing rows or columns comes in.

What Freezing Does:

- Keeps headers or labels visible while you scroll.
- Helps you stay oriented in large spreadsheets.
- Works for both horizontal and vertical navigation.

Think of it like pinning the top row or left column in place—so no matter how far you scroll, your reference points stay on screen.

2. HOW TO FREEZE ROWS OR COLUMNS

Step-by-Step to Freeze:

1. Click the View menu at the top.
2. Hover over Freeze.
3. Choose one of the following:
   » 1 row (to freeze just the header).
   » 2 rows (if you have multi-line headers).
   » Up to current row (based on your current selection).
   » Similarly, choose 1 column, 2 columns, or up to current.

Shortcut Option:

- Hover your mouse over the gray border between the column/row labels and the cell grid. You'll see a thick gray line appear.
- Click and drag that line down or to the right to freeze manually.

To Unfreeze:

- Go to View > Freeze > No rows or No columns.

	A	B	C	D	E	F
1	Category	Item	Quantity	Unit price	Cost	
2	Products	Laptop	1	$1,100.00	$1,100.00	
3	Products	Mouse	1	$35.00	$35.00	
4	Products	Headphones	1	$110.00	$110.00	
5	Products	Digital Drawing Tablet	1	$350.00	$350.00	Freeze row
6	Products	Printer	1	$250.00	$250.00	
7	Products	Notebooks	3	$10.00	$30.00	
8	Products	Pens	3	$2.00	$6.00	
9	Products	Printer paper	1	$10.00	$10.00	
10						
11		← Freeze column				

V. SORTING AND FILTERING DATA

When your spreadsheet starts to grow with lots of rows and columns, it becomes harder to find what you need. That's where sorting and filtering come in. They allow you to reorganize or narrow down your data in seconds—without changing the underlying structure.

1. FILTERING: SHOWING ONLY WHAT YOU NEED

Filters let you temporarily hide rows that don't match certain criteria—without deleting anything.

How to Turn On Filters:

1. Click anywhere in your data table.
2. Go to Data > Create a filter.
3. A filter icon will appear in each column header.

	A	B	C	D	E
1	Category	Item	Quantity	Unit price	Cost
2	Products	Digital Drawing Tablet	1	$350.00	$350.00
3	Products	Headphones	1	$110.00	$110.00
4	Products	Laptop	1	$1,100.00	$1,100.00
5	Products	Mouse	1	$35.00	$35.00
6	Products	Notebooks	3	$10.00	$30.00
7	Products	Pens	3	$2.00	$6.00
8	Products	Printer	1	$250.00	$250.00
9	Products	Printer paper	1	$10.00	$10.00

How to Apply a Filter:

1. Click the filter icon on the column you want to filter.
2. Choose from the following:
   » Specific values (e.g., only show "Groceries" or "Rent").
   » Conditions (e.g., greater than 100, text contains "overdue").
   » Filter by color (if conditional formatting was used).

Reset or Remove Filters:

- Click Data > Remove filter.
- Or clear the filter from individual columns by clicking the icon and choosing "Clear".

2. SORTING: ALPHABETICAL AND NUMERICAL

Sorting helps you view names alphabetically, rank items from highest to lowest (or vice versa) and group similar entries together.

How to Sort a Single Column:

1. Click the drop-down arrow in the column header (after turning on filters).
2. Select Sort A → Z for ascending (A to Z, 0 to 9). Or choose Sort Z → A for descending.

How to Sort a Whole Dataset:

1. Highlight the full table, including headers.
2. Go to Data > Sort range.
3. Check "Data has header row" if your first row contains labels.
4. Choose the column(s) to sort by, and the order.

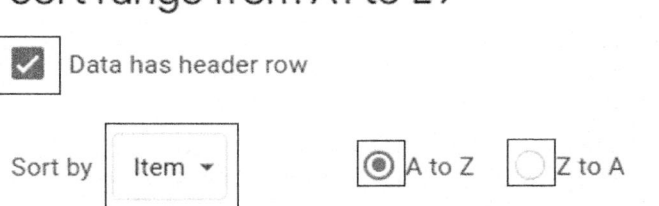

Important: Always select the full range of related columns—not just a single column—when sorting. Otherwise, your rows can become misaligned.

3. NEW TOOLBAR BUTTONS IN GOOGLE SHEETS 2026

Google Sheets added a row of quick-action buttons in the 2025–2026 interface to help you work faster without opening menus. These icons appear along the top toolbar and give you one-click access to common tools.

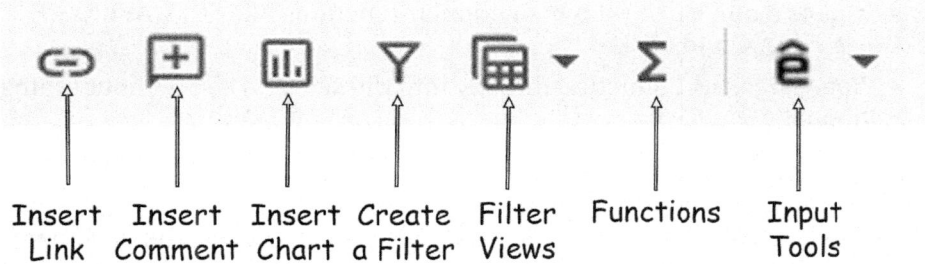

Insert Link

- Attaches a clickable link to the selected cell.
- Useful for referencing websites, documents, internal sheets, or any external resources.
- You can link to specific ranges, sheets, or headings to help teammates navigate quickly.

Insert Comment

- Adds a comment to the selected cell.
- Useful for notes, feedback, or assigning tasks to teammates.
- You can tag someone with @name and assign it as an action item.

Insert Chart

- Creates a chart instantly based on the data you selected.
- Google Sheets will suggest the most suitable chart
- ype, and you can switch to others from the sidebar.

Create a Filter

- Turns filters on or off in one click.
- When filters are active, the icon turns green.
- This is the fastest way to filter a table without going through the Data menu.

Filter Views

- Opens the filter views menu, where you can create custom filter views that don't affect how other collaborators see the sheet.
- Perfect for teams who need different ways to look at the same data.

Functions

- Opens a quick drop-down of popular functions like SUM, AVERAGE, COUNT, MAX, and MIN.
- You can insert a function directly into the selected cell without typing it manually.

Input Tools

- This icon lets you switch input methods, such as on-screen keyboards or special character tools.

- Useful if you're entering symbols, accented characters, or working on a touchscreen device.

VI. DATA VALIDATION AND DROP-DOWN LISTS

Have you ever shared a spreadsheet with someone, only to have them type in "Mondaay" instead of "Monday" or leave an important column blank? This is where Data Validation comes to the rescue.

It helps control what kind of data people can enter into a cell—reducing typos, inconsistencies, and headaches.

1. WHAT IS DATA VALIDATION?

Data validation is a feature that limits input to specific values or formats. It's especially helpful when: Creating dropdowns; ensuring only numbers or dates are entered; preventing errors in shared sheets.

2. CREATING A DROP-DOWN LIST

Let's create a drop-down menu for Staff list: "Male", "Female".

1. Select the cells where you want the dropdown (e.g., C2:C20).
2. Go to Insert > Dropdown or Data > Data validation.

3. Under Criteria, choose: Dropdown (or "List of items").
4. In the options box, type: Male, Female.
5. Click Done.

Now each selected cell will have a clickable arrow showing the drop-down menu.

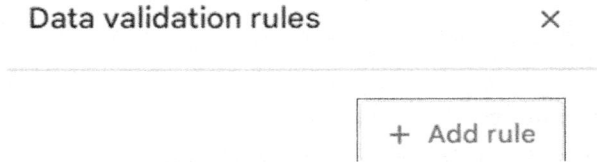

Visual Options (Bonus):

- Click on the dropdown cell.
- Click the paint palette icon to change how each choice is styled. Add color coding for each option (e.g., green for Done).

VII. HIDING, GROUPING & PROTECTING DATA

As your sheets grow in size and complexity, not all information needs to be visible—or editable—all the time. Google Sheets gives you simple but powerful ways to: Hide data you don't need to see right now; group rows or columns for collapsible sections; protect important ranges so collaborators can't accidentally break them.

1. HIDING ROWS AND COLUMNS

Sometimes, you just want to tuck certain data away—like archived items, helper columns, or reference info.

To Hide:

1. Select the row or column you want to hide.
2. Right-click > Hide row or Hide column.

You'll notice a small icon with arrows appear between the hidden rows or columns.

To Unhide:

1. Click the small arrow icon between the rows/columns.
2. Or select surrounding rows, right-click > Unhide.

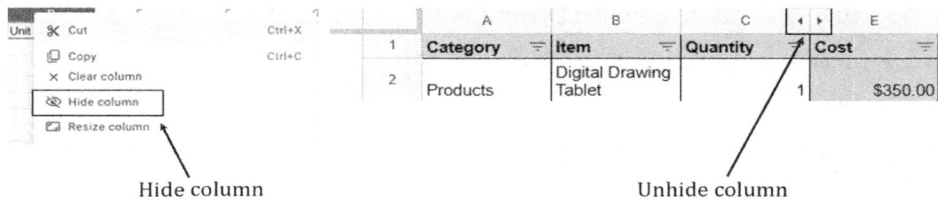

Hide column   Unhide column

2. GROUPING ROWS OR COLUMNS

Grouping lets you collapse and expand multiple rows or columns—perfect for organizing large datasets.

To Group Rows or Columns:

1. Select the rows or columns you want to group (e.g., rows 8-9). Right-click > Group rows 8-9.

2. A [-] button will appear on the left - click it to collapse the section.
3. It changes to [+] when collapsed - click to expand.

To Ungroup Rows or Columns:

	A	B	C	D	E
1	Category	Item	Quantity	Unit price	Cost
2	Products	Digital Drawing Tablet	1	$350.00	$350.00
6	Products	Notebooks	3	$10.00	$30.00
7	Products	Pens	3	$2.00	$6.00
8	Products	Printer paper	1	$10.00	$10.00
9	Products	Printer	1	$250.00	$250.00

1. Select grouped rows (with a +/- sign and gray bracket beside row numbers) or grouped columns (with a +/- sign and bracket above column letters).
2. Right-click > Remove Group.

3. PROTECTING DATA

If you're sharing your sheet and want to prevent accidental edits, you can lock down parts of it while still letting others use or view the file.

To Protect a Range or Sheet:

1. Select the range or sheet tab you want to protect.
2. Go to Data > Protect sheets and ranges.
3. In the sidebar:
   » Add a description.
   » Select range or entire sheet.
4. Click Set permissions:
   » Choose who can or can't edit.
   » Limit to just yourself, or specific editors.

37

Use Cases: Lock formula columns so users don't overwrite them; protect dashboard layouts; restrict access to financial data while allowing input on basic fields.

Tip: You can show a warning instead of blocking edits. This is less strict but still signals that an area is sensitive.

With your data now organized, collapsible, and protected, you're ready to put it all into practice with a real-world formatting challenge!

VIII. PRACTICE EXERCISE – ORGANIZE THIS SHEET!

You've learned how to format, structure, and clean up your data like a pro. Now it's time to test those skills in a real-world scenario.

Imagine you've been handed the following spreadsheet:

	A	B	C	D
1	item	Quantity	Category	status
2	apples	4	groceries	bought
3	shampoo	2	hygiene	
4	Bread	1	Groceries	BOUGHT
5	toothpaste		Hygiene	bought
6	Chicken	3	groceries	not yet

It's not great. Your task is to organize this sheet using the tools you've learned, transforming it into something clean, readable, and usable.

Step-by-Step Instructions:

1. Fix the Headers:
   » Capitalize consistently: Item, Quantity, Category, Status.
   » Bold and center-align them.

2. Clean the Data:
   » Standardize capitalization (BOUGHT → Bought).
   » Fill missing values or mark with "N/A" or 0.
   » Format text and numbers properly.

3. Apply Conditional Formatting:
   » Highlight rows where Status is "Not Yet" in light red.
   » Mark rows with missing quantity in yellow.

4. Add a Drop-Down for Status:
   » Options: Bought, Not Yet, Need to Check.

5. Wrap Text in Item Column:
   » Prevent cutoff for longer item names.
6. Freeze the Header Row.
7. Add Borders and Colors:
   » Use light background shading for headers.
   » Add clean grid borders to the table.

	A	B	C	D	E
1	**Item**	**Quantity**	**Category**	**Status**	
2	Apples	4	Groceries	Bought ▼	
3	Shampoo	2	Hygiene	▼	
4	Bread	1	Groceries	Bought ▼	
5	Toothpaste		Hygiene	Bought ▼	
6	Chicken	3	Groceries	Not Yet ▼	
7					
8				Bought	
9					
10				Not Yet	
11					
12				Need to Check	

IX. TIPS AND BEST PRACTICES

After applying all the formatting techniques, you want to make sure your spreadsheet stays clean, readable, and professional—especially if others will view or use it.

- Use Styles Consistently:
  » One or two font types per sheet.
  » A matching color palette for headers, highlights, and borders.
  » Consistent font size for similar elements (e.g., body text = 10pt).

- Keep It Clean:
  » Use white space to break sections visually.
  » Add borders sparingly to create structure.
  » Use conditional formatting to draw attention, not overwhelm.

- Always Preview Before Sharing or Printing:
  » Go to File > Print.
  » Use "Fit to width" or "Fit to page" under Scaling.
  » Check margins, column widths, and headers.

- Add a title row or sheet name at the top of printed versions for clarity.

- Empty Cell Detection Improvements: Google Sheets now detects "empty-looking" cells that actually contain:
  » Inconsistent spaces.
  » Invisible characters.
  » Imported formatting artifacts.
  » Smart Cleanup will flag these under "Fix inconsistent whitespace."

This makes data cleaning faster, especially for sheets created from copied or imported data.

CHAPTER 3: ESSENTIAL FORMULAS AND FUNCTIONS

I. INTRODUCTION TO FORMULAS

1. WHAT ARE FORMULAS?

At the core of any powerful spreadsheet lies the ability to perform calculations automatically. This is where formulas come in. A formula is an equation or set of instructions that allows Google Sheets to perform calculations, manipulate data, and produce results - all without you manually adding numbers.

A formula always starts with an equal sign (=), followed by the function name (SUM, AVERAGE, etc.) and any necessary arguments (values, cell ranges, etc.). It can be as simple or as complex as you need it to be.

Simple Formula Example:

If you want to add two numbers in cells A1 and A2, the formula would be:

=A1+A2.

Google Sheets would instantly calculate the sum of the two numbers.

2. WHERE TO WRITE FORMULAS

Option 1: The Formula Bar

Located at the top, just below the menu bar. This is where you write or edit formulas directly.

Option 2: Directly in the Cell

Select the cell where you want the result, and start typing the formula there. Google Sheets will automatically calculate and display the result in the same cell.

Tip: Use the Formula Bar if you're working with complex formulas to make sure everything is clear and easy to read.

3. PARTS OF A FORMULA

Let's break down a formula to understand its structure. We'll use the following example:

=SUM(A1:A10)

1. Equal Sign (=) – Every formula begins with an equal sign, telling Google Sheets that you're about to enter a formula.
2. Function Name (SUM) – This tells Google Sheets what operation to perform (in this case, adding up all the values in a range).
3. Arguments (A1:A10) – These are the values or ranges that the function works with. Here, it's the range of cells from A1 to A10.
4. Arguments can be:
   » Cell references (e.g., A1, B3, C5).
   » Ranges (e.g., A1:A10, B2:D5).
   » Numbers (e.g., 5, 100).
   » Text (e.g., "Hello").

E11 fx =SUM(E2:E10)

	A	B	C	D	E
1	Category	Item	Quantity	Unit price	Cost
2	Products	Digital Drawing Tablet	1	$350.00	$350.00
3	Products	Stylus pens	1	$19.82	$19.82
4	Products	Headphones	1	$110.00	$110.00
5	Products	Laptop	1	$1,100.00	$1,100.00
6	Products	Mouse	1	$35.00	$35.00
7	Products	Notebooks	3	$10.00	$30.00
8	Products	Pens	3	$2.00	$6.00
9	Products	Printer paper	1	$10.00	$10.00
10	Products	Printer	1	$250.00	$250.00
11					$1,910.82

4. How Formulas Work

When you press Enter, Google Sheets processes the formula and returns the result in the selected cell. The formula doesn't "disappear" - you can still see it in the formula bar or cell if you click on it.

Formulas are dynamic - this means they update automatically when the referenced data changes. For example, if you change the value in A1, the result of =SUM(A1:A10) will automatically recalculate.

With these basics in hand, you're ready to jump into more powerful formulas in the next sections, where we'll cover the most essential functions you'll use day in and day out—starting with the basic math functions in the next section.

5. Formula Suggestions (AI-Assisted 2025–2026)

Google Sheets now includes formula suggestions powered by AI. When you type into a cell, Sheets may display a faint suggestion (ghost text) or a blue popup recommending a formula based on patterns in your data.

These suggestions can:

- Identify the correct function automatically.
- Recommend SUM, AVERAGE, COUNT, MAX, MIN.
- Suggest VLOOKUP or INDEX/MATCH automatically.
- Spot columns that can be combined with TEXTJOIN.
- Suggest SPLIT when it detects delimited text.

Press Tab to accept a suggestion or Esc to ignore it.

	A	B
1	154	
2	5487	
3	581	
4	3154	
5	84	
6	18	
7	6597	
8	=SUM(A1:A7)	
9	Tab SUM(A1:A7)	16075
10		

This helps beginners avoid typing entire formulas manually and reduces mistakes.

II. AUTO-FILL AND SMART FORMULA TOOLS

Google Sheets isn't just powerful - it's smart. It can recognize patterns, suggest formulas, and automatically fill in values or calculations to save you time. In this section, you'll learn how to use:

- Auto-Fill (to quickly apply formulas or values to multiple cells).
- Smart suggestions from Google Sheets.
- Relative vs Absolute references (an essential concept for copying formulas without breaking them).

1. USING AUTO-FILL

Auto-Fill is a quick way to copy a value or formula down a column or across a row without typing or pasting manually.

How to Use Auto-Fill:

1. Enter a value or formula in a cell (e.g., =A1+B1).
2. Hover your mouse over the bottom-right corner of the cell. You'll see a small blue square - this is the fill handle.
3. Click and drag it down (or across) to fill the rest of the cells.

Google Sheets will automatically copy and adjust the formula based on its position (we'll explain how in the next subsection).

Example:

If A1=1 and B1=2, and you type =A1+B1 in C1, then auto-fill it down to C3:

- C2 will become =A2+B2.
- C3 will become =A3+B3.

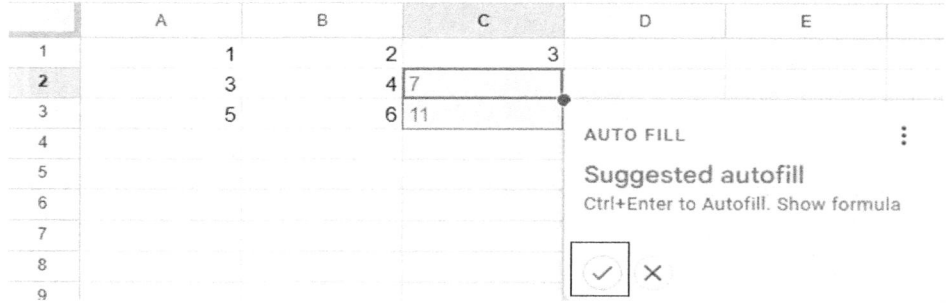

Pro Tip: Double-click the fill handle to auto-fill all the way down the column as long as the adjacent column has data.

2. RELATIVE VS ABSOLUTE CELL REFERENCES

When you copy a formula, Google Sheets adjusts the cell references relative to their new positions. This is called a relative reference. But sometimes, you want to lock a reference in place so it doesn't change. That's where absolute references come in. Let's break it down:

Relative Reference (default):

» Formula: =A1+B1
» When copied down one row → becomes =A2+B2.

Absolute Reference:
- » Formula: =$A$1+$B$1
- » When copied down → still refers to A1 and B1.

The dollar signs $ freeze the reference:
- » $A$1: locks both the column and the row.
- » A$1: locks the row, but column can change.
- » $A1: locks the column, but row can change.

Example:

Let's say you want to apply a 10% tax to a list of prices in column A.

1. You store the tax rate in cell B1.
2. In cell B2, you write: =A2*$B$1
3. You use $B$1 to lock the tax rate, so when you drag the formula down, it doesn't change to $B$2, $B$3, etc.

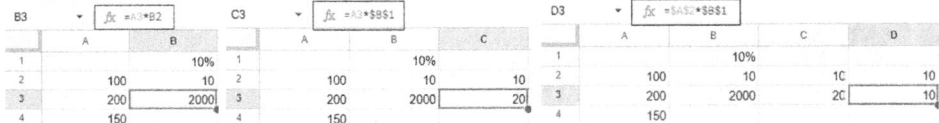

Quick Reference Chart:

Reference Type	Example	What It Does
Relative	A1	Changes with movement
Absolute	$A$1	Fixed row & column
Mixed	A$1 or $A1	Fixes either row or column only

Understanding how references work is crucial when building dynamic spreadsheets. Without this, your formulas may break when copied—so it's a good habit to double-check your references as you go.

Formula Correction Assistant:

When a formula doesn't work, Google Sheets now opens an "Error Assistant" panel automatically.

This panel explains what caused the error.

This makes troubleshooting much easier, especially for beginners.

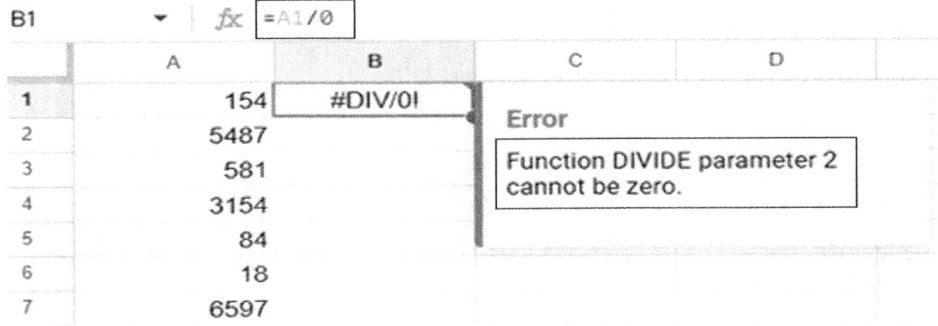

III. BASIC MATH FUNCTIONS EVERYONE SHOULD KNOW

Google Sheets comes with built-in functions that make math super simple. In this section, we'll cover the five most-used functions: SUM, AVERAGE, COUNT, MAX, MIN.

1. SUM – ADD IT UP

The SUM function totals up all the values in a range of cells.

Syntax:

=SUM(range)

Example: Let's say you have values in cells A1 to A5:

Type this in any other cell:

=SUM(A1:A5). You'll get: 50.

Use Cases: Total monthly expenses; total points scored; total hours worked.

2. AVERAGE

The AVERAGE function calculates the average of a group of numbers.

Syntax:

=AVERAGE(range)

Example:

=AVERAGE(A1:A5) would return 10, because (10+15+12+8+5)÷5 = 10.

Use Cases: Student test scores; daily step counts; average sales per week.

46

3. COUNT – COUNT HOW MANY NUMBERS

The COUNT function tells you how many numeric values exist in a range.

Syntax:

=COUNT(range)

Example:

=COUNT(A1:A5)

It would return 3 since it ignores the text and blank cell.

	A
1	10
2	15
3	"apple"
4	12
5	

Variants:

- COUNTA: counts everything (numbers + text).
- COUNTBLANK: counts empty cells.

4. MAX – GET THE HIGHEST NUMBER

The MAX function returns the largest value in a range.

Syntax:

=MAX(range)

Example:

=MAX(A1:A5) → 15

	A
1	10
2	15
3	12
4	8
5	5

Use Cases: Highest test score; peak sales day; top-performing product.

5. MIN – GET THE SMALLEST NUMBER

The MIN function returns the smallest value in a range.

Syntax:

=MIN(range)

Example (same dataset as the Max formula example).

=MIN(A1:A5) → 5

Use Cases: Lowest score; smallest expense; minimum temperature.

Practice Table:

Let's create a small dataset to practice with:

	A	B
1	Day	Sales ($)
2	Monday	$100.00
3	Tuesday	$150.00
4	Wednesday	$75.00
5	Thursday	$200.00
6	Friday	$125.00

Try these formulas:

- =SUM(B2:B6) → Total sales for the week.
- =AVERAGE(B2:B6) → Average daily sales.
- =MAX(B2:B6) → Highest sales day.
- =MIN(B2:B6) → Lowest sales day.
- =COUNT(B2:B6) → Number of days with data.

Tip: Combine these functions with conditional formatting to create dynamic dashboards that automatically highlight your highs and lows.

6. USING THE FUNCTIONS SIDEBAR

Google Sheets now includes a dedicated Functions Sidebar that appears when you click Insert → Function.

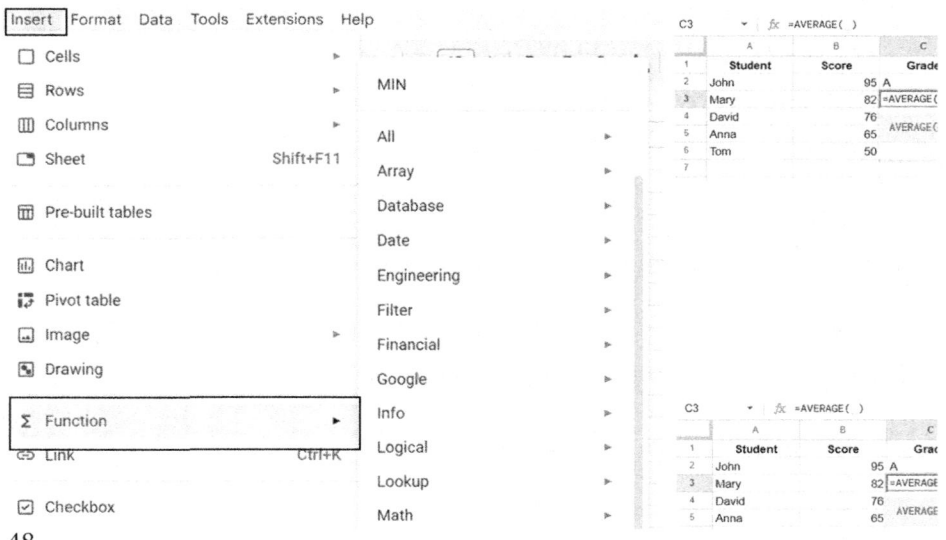

It includes:

- Function descriptions.
- Required arguments.
- Examples.
- Live previews.
- A search bar for finding the right formula.

When you click a function, Sheets inserts the structure (for example: =AVERAGE()) and highlights the expected input range.

This sidebar is useful for users learning new formulas without needing to memorize syntax.

IV. UNDERSTANDING FORMULA ERRORS

Even experienced spreadsheet users occasionally see strange error codes pop up instead of expected results. Google Sheets does a good job of flagging problems, but understanding what the error means (and how to fix it) will save you a lot of frustration.

1. COMMON ERRORS AND WHAT THEY MEAN

Let's decode the most common formula errors you'll see in Google Sheets:

Error	What It Means	How to Fix It
#REF!	A cell reference is broken (e.g., deleted cell or row)	Double-check the range or undo the deletion
#DIV/0!	You're dividing by zero, which isn't allowed	Make sure the denominator isn't zero or blank
#VALUE!	You're mixing text with numbers or using the wrong type of input	Check your function arguments or data types
#N/A	The formula can't find a value (often in VLOOKUP or MATCH)	Confirm that the lookup value exists and matches
#ERROR!	Syntax or function error—something is wrong with how the formula is written	Review parentheses, commas, or quotes
#NAME?	The formula uses an unknown function or misspelling	Double-check your function name (e.g., =SOM() instead of =SUM())

2. How to Troubleshoot Formulas

When in doubt, use this checklist:

1. Click the Cell: Click the cell showing the error to view the formula in the Formula Bar.
2. Break the Formula Down:
   » Split long formulas into smaller pieces.
   » Test one part at a time.
3. Use the Function Tooltip: As you type, Google Sheets shows tooltips with required arguments and suggestions.
4. Highlight Input Ranges: Click the formula - color-coded highlights will show you exactly which cells are being used.

3. Use IFERROR() to Keep Things Clean

The IFERROR() function helps you handle errors gracefully, without showing ugly codes in your reports or dashboards.

Syntax:

=IFERROR(original_formula, "Custom message or fallback value")

Example:

Instead of showing #DIV/0!, write:

=IFERROR(A1/B1, "Check denominator")

This will display "Check denominator" when B1 is zero or empty, instead of an error.

Practice Table: Common Errors in Action

A	B	C
10	2	=A1/B1 → 5
10	0	=A2/B2 → #DIV/0!
Apple	5	=A3+B3 → #VALUE!
		=SOM(A1:A3) → #NAME?

If the IFERROR function is used, the result is:

	A	B	C
			fx =IFERROR(A2/B2,"Check denominator")
1	10	2	5
2	10	0	Check denominator
3	Apple	5	Check denominator
4			Check denominator

Tip: When sharing sheets with clients, teachers, or teammates, always use IFERROR() to keep things tidy and professional.

4. EXPLAIN FORMULA (GEMINI INTEGRATION)

Google Sheets now includes an "Explain formula" option powered by Gemini.

Click a formula, Sheets will generate:

- A plain-language explanation.
- Step-by-step logic.
- What each argument does.
- Example outputs.
- Suggestions for improvement.

This feature is helpful when you're learning new formulas or reviewing someone else's work.

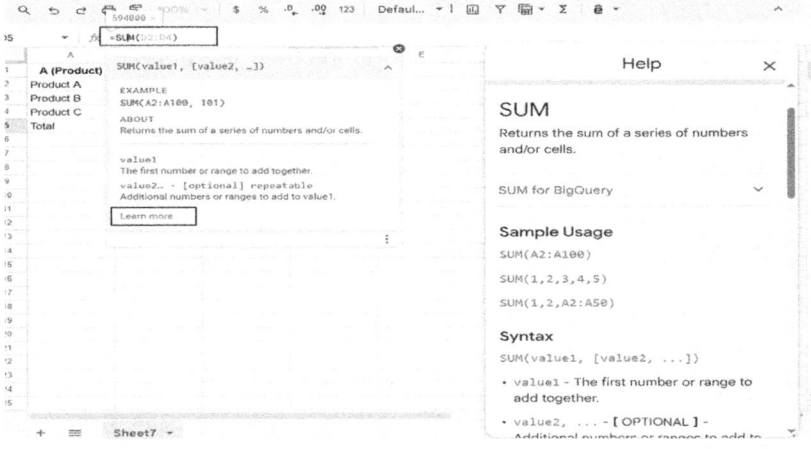

51

V. TIPS FOR BEGINNERS USING FORMULAS

Formulas don't have to be intimidating. In fact, Google Sheets gives you plenty of built-in tools to make working with functions easier, faster, and (dare we say it?) more fun. This section covers:

- Using the function menu.
- Taking advantage of tooltips and auto-complete.
- Organizing with named ranges and cell comments.

1. USE THE FUNCTION MENU (THE Σ BUTTON)

When you're not sure what formula to use, or how to start typing it, let the Function Menu help you.

How to Use It:

1. Click the cell where you want the result.
2. Click the Function (Σ) icon on the toolbar.

3. Alternatively, find it under: Insert > Function.
4. Choose a function from one of the categories:
   » Math (e.g., SUM, AVERAGE).
   » Logical (IF, AND, OR).
   » Lookup (VLOOKUP, MATCH).
   » Text, Date, Database, and more.

Tip: Use this to discover new functions you haven't tried before!

2. USE TOOLTIPS AND AUTO-COMPLETE

As soon as you start typing a formula (e.g., =S), Google Sheets will suggest matching functions and show you how they work.

The Tooltip Window:

- Shows the syntax of the function.
- Lists each argument needed.
- Often includes helpful examples.

Example:

After you type =AVERAGE(Google Sheets will show:

=AVERAGE(value1, [value2, ...])

and explains that it calculates the mean of selected values.

Just click the suggested formula or hit Tab to auto-complete it.

	A	B	C
1	10		
2	15		
3	12		
4	8		
5	5		
6	=AVERAGE(A1:A5)		
7	AVERAGE(A1:A5) ← The Tooltip Window		10
8			

Tip: If you're not sure what a function does, hover over the name in the tooltip - it often includes a short description.

3. STAY ORGANIZED WITH NAMED RANGES AND COMMENTS

When formulas get long or refer to multiple places, naming your ranges and adding notes helps you (and others) stay sane.

i. Named Ranges

In your formula, instead of using A1:A20, give that range a name like SalesData.

How to Create:

1. Select your range.
2. Go to Data > Named ranges.
3. Give it a descriptive name (no spaces allowed!).
4. Then use it in your formula: =SUM(SalesData).

Named ranges make formulas easier to read and maintain.

ii. Cell Comments

Sometimes it's helpful to explain what a formula is doing, especially when working with collaborators.

1. Right-click the cell. Choose Comment.
2. Add a description or reminder (e.g., "This formula adds Q1 totals")

	A	B	C	D	E
1	Product	Sales Q1	Sales Q2	Sales Q3	Sales Q4
2	Product A	500	600	700	650
3	Product B	300	400	500	550
4	Product C	400	450	600	620
5		1200			

B5 fx =SUM(SalesData)

This formula adds Q1 totals

VI. QUICK CHALLENGES FOR PRACTICE

Now that you've mastered basic formulas, it's time to put your skills to the test. These short exercises are designed to reinforce everything from SUM to MAX, with real-life-style data.

1. CHALLENGE 1: CALCULATE TOTAL AND AVERAGE GRADES

Student	Score 1	Score 2	Total	Average
Mia	85	90		
Leo	78	82		
Ava	92	88		
Eli	65	70		
Zoe	100	95		

Task:

- Calculate each student's total score and their average score.
- Highlight students with an average below 75 using conditional formatting.

Results:

	A	B	C	D	E
1	Student	Score 1	Score 2	Total	Average
2	Mia	85	90	175	87.5
3	Leo	78	82	160	80
4	Ava	92	88	180	90
5	Eli	65	70	135	67.5
6	Zoe	100	95	195	97.5

2. **CHALLENGE 2: COUNT HOW MANY SALES EXCEED TARGET**

Product	Units Sold	Target
Apples	120	100
Bananas	85	100
Oranges	130	100
Grapes	150	100
Berries	95	100

TASK:

- Count how many products sold more than 100 units.
- Find the product with the highest and lowest sales.

Results:

	A	B	C	D
1	Product	Units Sold	Target	
2	Apples	120	100	
3	Bananas	85	100	
4	Oranges	130	100	
5	Grapes	150	100	
6	Berries	95	100	
7	Count products that sold more than 100 units	3	←——— =COUNTIF(B2:B6,">100")	
8	Find the highest sales figure	150	←——— =MAX(B2:B6)	
9	Find the lowest sales figure	85	←——— =MIN(B2:B6)	

3. Challenge 3: Identify Best and Worst Product Ratings

Product	Rating
Notebook	4.3
Pen	3.9
Marker	4.7
Stapler	3.5
Tape	4.0

Task:

- Identify the highest-rated product and the lowest-rated product.
- Mark the statuses of the products, in which: "Top" for ratings ≥ 4.5, "OK" for ratings between 4.0–4.4, "Low" for anything below 4.0.

Formula:

=IF(B2>=4.5,"Top",IF(B2>=4,"OK","Low"))

C2   fx =IF(B2>=4.5,"Top",IF(B2>=4,"OK","Low"))

	A	B	C	D
1	Product	Rating	Status	
2	Notebook	4.3	OK	
3	Pen	3.9	Low	
4	Marker	4.7	Top	
5	Stapler	3.5	Low	
6	Tape	4	OK	
7	Highest Rating	4.7	←——— =MAX(B2:B6)	
8	Lowest Rating	3.5	←——— =MIN(B2:B6)	

These mini-projects are not only great for practice - they mimic real-world uses you'll encounter again and again in school, business, freelancing, and beyond.

CHAPTER 4: LOGICAL & LOOKUP FUNCTIONS

I. INTRODUCTION TO LOGICAL THINKING IN SHEETS

Up to now, you've been using Google Sheets to do math and organize data. But what if your spreadsheet could make decisions based on the data it holds? That's what logical functions do—they evaluate conditions and return results based on whether something is true or false.

1. WHAT ARE LOGICAL FUNCTIONS?

Logical functions help your spreadsheet: Ask questions about your data (Is this item over 100? Out of stock?); make decisions based on the answers; return specific values depending on what's true.

These are some of the most common:

- IF – The foundation of all logic formulas.
- AND – Checks if **all** conditions are true.
- OR – Checks if **any** condition is true.
- NOT – Reverses a condition (e.g., "if NOT empty").

2. WHY USE LOGIC IN SPREADSHEETS?

Logical functions are incredibly useful when you want your sheet to do more than just calculate—it should be able to respond, flag issues, or give you answers without manual checks.

Real-Life Examples:

Use Case	Logic Applied
Grading System	If score ≥ 60 → "Pass" else "Fail"
Inventory Alert	If stock ≤ 10 → "Low Stock"
Payment Tracker	If paid = "Yes" → Leave blank, else → "Send Reminder"
Time Tracker	If hours > 8 → "Overtime"

Your spreadsheet is like a robot that can only understand logic. You have to speak its language using conditions, like: "IF this thing is true, then do this. ELSE, do something else."

That's the foundation of everything we'll cover in this chapter.

II. THE IF FUNCTION (AND ITS FRIENDS)

The IF function is one of the most useful and versatile formulas in Google Sheets. It allows you to return different values based on whether a condition is true or false.

1. IF FUNCTION – THE BASICS

The IF function gives your spreadsheet a yes/no question to answer.

Syntax:

=IF(condition, value_if_true, value_if_false)

Example Table:

Name	Score
Mia	85
Leo	68
Ava	90
Eli	55

Task: Check if students pass or fail based on their scores. If score ≥ 70, pass, else fail.

Formula in C2:

=IF(B2>=70, "Pass", "Fail")

	A	B	C
1	Name	Score	Result (IF Formula)
2	Mia	85	Pass
3	Leo	68	Fail
4	Ava	90	Pass
5	Eli	55	Fail

2. NESTING IF STATEMENTS

Want more than just "Pass" or "Fail"? You can nest IF functions inside each other to create more options.

Example: Letter Grades

=IF(A2>=90,"A",IF(A2>=80,"B",IF(A2>=70,"C","F")))

This formula:

- Returns **A** if 90 or above.
- Returns **B** if 80–89.
- Returns **C** if 70–79.
- Returns **F** if below 70.

	A	B	C	D
1	Score	Grade		
2	95	A		
3	84	B		
4	73	C		
5	61	F		

3. AND, OR, NOT FUNCTIONS

These are supporting logic functions that help you build more powerful conditions.

i. AND Function

Returns TRUE only if all conditions are true.

Example:

=AND(A2>70, B2<100)

→ TRUE only if A2 is greater than 70 and B2 is less than 100.

ii. OR Function

Returns TRUE if any one of the conditions is true.

Example:

=OR(A2="Admin", A2="Manager")

→ TRUE if A2 is either Admin or Manager.

iii. NOT Function

Reverses a condition—TRUE becomes FALSE and vice versa.

Example:

=NOT(A2="Complete")

→ TRUE if A2 is not equal to "Complete".

4. COMBINING IF WITH AND/OR

You can nest logical functions inside an IF to make smarter decisions.

Example:

=IF(AND(A2>70, B2<100), "Valid", "Check")

This will:

- Return **"Valid"** only if A2 is over 70 **and** B2 is under 100.
- Otherwise, it returns **"Check"**.

Real-Life Use Case: Task Status Check

Task	Status	Due in Days	Flag (Formula)
Report	Complete	2	No Action Needed
Slides	Not Started	1	Urgent!
Budget	In Progress	5	Monitor

Formula in D2:

=IF(B2="Complete", "No Action Needed", IF(C2<=2, "Urgent!", "Monitor"))

or

=IF(B2="Complete", "No Action Needed", IF(OR(C2<=2, AND(B2="Not Started", D2="High")), "Urgent!", "Monitor"))

5. USING IFS FOR CLEANER MULTI-CONDITION LOGIC

Google Sheets includes the IFS function, which evaluates multiple conditions without needing to nest IF statements.

Syntax:

=IFS(condition1, value1, condition2, value2, ...)

Example:

	A	B	C	D	E
			fx =IFS(B2>=90,"A",B2>=80,"B",B2>=70,"C",B2>=60,"D",TRUE,"F")		
1	Student	Score	Grade		
2	John	95	A		
3	Mary	82			
4	David	76			
5	Anna	65			
6	Tom	50			

The first TRUE condition wins.

IFS makes your formulas shorter and easier to read compared to deeply nested IF statements.

III. LOOKUP FUNCTIONS THAT FIND YOUR DATA

When your data grows into multiple rows and columns, it can be a pain to manually match things up. Lookup functions let Google Sheets find the information you want—instantly and automatically.

Whether you're looking up a product price, a student grade, or a team member's contact info, these tools are lifesavers. In this section, we'll cover: VLOOKUP, HLOOKUP, INDEX + MATCH, and LOOKUP.

1. WHAT ARE LOOKUP FUNCTIONS?

Lookup functions search a table or range for a value and return a related piece of information. They're the digital version of asking your spreadsheet:

"Hey, what's the price for product X?" or "Who got the top score in this list?"

Let's explore the most popular options.

2. VLOOKUP – VERTICAL LOOKUP

The superstar of lookup functions. It searches down a column and returns data from the same row in another column.

Syntax:

=VLOOKUP(search_key, range, index, [is_sorted])

Example: Let's say you have this product table:

Product	Price
Apple	1.00
Banana	0.50
Orange	0.75

In another cell, type:

=VLOOKUP("Banana", A2:B4, 2, FALSE)

Result: 0.50.

(Google Sheets looks for "Banana" in column A and returns the price from column 2).

Tips for Using VLOOKUP:

- The search value must be in the first column of your range.
- The index number refers to the column number inside the range.
- Use FALSE for exact matches (almost always!).

3. Lookup Using the FILTER Function (Modern Alternative to VLOOKUP)

Many Google Sheets experts now prefer using FILTER instead of VLOOKUP because it is more flexible and doesn't require the lookup column to be the first column.

Syntax:

=FILTER(return_range, lookup_range = value)

Example:

	A	B	C
		fx =FILTER(B2:B4,A2:A4="Banana")	
1	Product	Price	
2	Apple	1	
3	Banana	0.5	
4	Orange	0.75	
5			
6			
7		0.5	

Why FILTER is useful:

- No "column index number" required.
- Works left-to-right AND right-to-left.
- Automatically returns all matching results.
- Easier to maintain.

This is the recommended method for lookups when your data structure may change.

4. HLOOKUP – Horizontal Lookup

Just like VLOOKUP, but it searches across rows instead of columns.

Syntax:

=HLOOKUP(search_key, range, index, [is_sorted])

Example:

	A	B	C
Name	Mia	Leo	Ava
Score	90	85	92

Formula:

=HLOOKUP("Mia", A1:C2, 2, FALSE)

Result: 90.

(HLOOKUP looks for "Score" in the first row and returns the 2nd row value under column A).

D4 ▼ fx =HLOOKUP("Mia", A1:C2, 2, FALSE)

	A	B	C	D
1	Name	Mia	Leo	Ava
2	Score	90	85	92
3				
4				90

5. USING INDEX WITH FILTER (ADVANCED LOOKUP PATTERN)

You can combine INDEX + FILTER to return a single value from multiple matches.

Example:

=INDEX(FILTER(B2:B4, A2:A4="Apple"), 1)

This returns the first matching result, but still lets you keep flexible ranges.

B6 ▼ fx =INDEX(FILTER(B2:B4, A2:A4="Apple"), 1)

	A	B	C	D
1	Product	Price		
2	Apple	1		
3	Banana	0.5		
4	Orange	0.75		
5				
6		1		

This pattern is now widely used as a modern replacement for VLOOKUP.

6. INDEX + MATCH – THE SMARTER ALTERNATIVE

This combo is more flexible than VLOOKUP and doesn't require the search value to be in the first column.

How it Works:

- MATCH() finds the row number of your search value.
- INDEX() returns the value from that row and column.

Example:

Name	Department
Mia	Sales
Leo	Marketing
Ava	HR

To look up Leo's department:

=INDEX(B2:B4, MATCH("Leo", A2:A4, 0))

- MATCH("Leo", A2:A4, 0) returns 2 (Leo is in the 2nd row)
- INDEX(B2:B4, 2) returns "Marketing".

Why INDEX + MATCH is Better Than VLOOKUP

Feature	VLOOKUP	INDEX + MATCH
Needs search value in 1st column	✓ Yes	✗ No
Works left to right only	✓ Yes	✗ No (can go both ways)
Slower with large data	✗ Yes (sometimes)	✓ Faster
More flexible with column order	✗ No	✓ Yes

7. LOOKUP FUNCTION (BONUS)

LOOKUP() is a simpler version of VLOOKUP for sorted data only.

Syntax:

=LOOKUP(search_key, search_range, result_range)

Example:

=LOOKUP(85, A2:A6, B2:B6)

- Looks for the value just below or equal to 85 in column A.
- Returns the matching value from column B.

Tip: Use this only when your search column is sorted in ascending order.

IV. ADVANCED LOOKUP TOOLS

You've now mastered VLOOKUP and INDEX + MATCH—but what if you want to: Reference another sheet using a dynamic name; generate a cell address using row/column numbers; or even combine these techniques for more automated workflows?

That's what this section is about.

1. INDIRECT FUNCTION

The INDIRECT function returns a reference from a string. This lets you dynamically build a cell or range reference using text.

Syntax:

=INDIRECT(cell_reference_as_text)

Example:

=INDIRECT("Sheet2!A1")

This pulls the value from cell A1 in Sheet2, even if you don't directly reference it in the formula.

Real Use Case:

If cell A1 contains the word "Sheet2", this formula:

=INDIRECT(A1 & "!B2") will get the value in cell B2 of Sheet2, based on the name in A1.

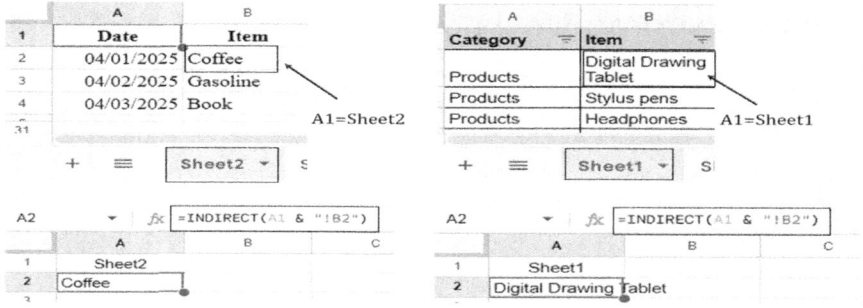

2. ADDRESS Function

The ADDRESS function returns a cell reference as text, based on the row and column numbers you give it.

Syntax:

=ADDRESS(row_num, column_num)

Example:

=ADDRESS(2, 3)

Returns: "C2" (because column 3 = column C).

You can use ADDRESS() when you want to generate cell references programmatically, and then combine it with INDIRECT() to actually pull the data.

Example (Combined with INDIRECT):

=INDIRECT(ADDRESS(2, 3)) → pulls the value from C2

Tip: This combo gives you flexibility to build references dynamically.

	A	B	C
1	10	20	30
2	15	25	35
3	18	28	38
4	Enter Row:	Enter Column:	Value:
5	2	3	35
6			

3. Real-Life Use Case: Cross-Sheet Lookups

Let's say you have monthly sales data on different sheets (January, February, March...). You want to build a dashboard that references a different sheet based on a drop-down selection.

Here's how:

1. Create a drop-down menu in A1 with sheet names (e.g., "January").
2. Use this formula in B1: =INDIRECT(A1 & "!B2")

3. It will:
   » Look at A1 (say it says "January").
   » Pull value from cell B2 in that sheet.

4. **Summary of When to Use Each**

Function	Best For
INDIRECT()	Dynamic sheet or cell referencing
ADDRESS()	Generating cell references from numbers
INDIRECT() + ADDRESS()	Creating dynamic references from calculations
Cross-Sheet Lookup	Pulling values based on user input or sheet name

V. PRACTICAL SCENARIOS AND PROJECTS

You've now got the skills to build smarter spreadsheets—so let's build some mini projects together. These examples combine IF, AND, OR, VLOOKUP, INDEX + MATCH, and conditional formatting in practical, ready-to-use ways.

1. Build a Grading System with Nested IFs

Use Case: Convert numerical scores to letter grades based on cutoffs.

Student	Score	Grade
Mia	92	
Leo	83	
Ava	76	
Eli	61	

Formula:

=IF(B2>=90,"A",IF(B2>=80,"B",IF(B2>=70,"C",IF(B2>=60,"D","F"))))

	A	B	C	D	E	F
1	Student	Score	Grade			
2	Mia	92	A			
3	Leo	83	B			
4	Ava	76	C			
5	Eli	61	D			

Bonus: Use conditional formatting to highlight "A" grades in green and highlight "F" grades in red.

2. BUILD A SIMPLE EMPLOYEE LOOKUP TOOL

Enter an employee's name and automatically pull their department, title, or salary.

	A	B	C	D
1	**Name**	**Department**	**Title**	**Salary**
2	Mia	Sales	Manager	80,000
3	Leo	Marketing	Analyst	70,000
4	Ava	HR	Coordinator	65,000

In your lookup area:

	A	B	C	D
1	**Name**	**Department**	**Title**	**Salary**
2	Mia	Sales	Manager	80,000
3	Leo	Marketing	Analyst	70,000
4	Ava	HR	Coordinator	65,000
5				
6	**Search Name**	Ava		
7	Department	(formula)		
8	Title	(formula)		
9	Salary	(formula)		

Formula (using INDEX + MATCH):

B7   *fx* `=INDEX(B2:B4, MATCH(B6, A2:A4, 0))`

	A	B	C	D
1	**Name**	**Department**	**Title**	**Salary**
2	Mia	Sales	Manager	80,000
3	Leo	Marketing	Analyst	70,000
4	Ava	HR	Coordinator	65,000
5				
6	**Search Name**	Ava	← Search_key	
7	Department	HR		
8	Title	Coordinator		

=INDEX(B2:B4, MATCH(B6, A2:A4, 0)) → for Department eg. HR.

=INDEX(C2:C4, MATCH(B6, A2:A4, 0)) → for Title eg. Coordinator.

=INDEX(D2:D4, MATCH(B6, A2:A4, 0)) → for Salary eg. 65,000.

3. BUDGET ALERT SYSTEM WITH LOGIC

Use Case:

Flag budget categories that go over their spending limits.

Category	Limit	Spent	Status
Food	300	275	
Rent	1000	1000	
Travel	150	200	

Formula:

=IF(C2>B2, "Over Budget", IF(C2=B2, "At Limit", "OK"))

Bonus:

Add icons or color using conditional formatting: Red = Over Budget, Yellow = At Limit, Green = OK.

	A	B	C	D	E
1	Category	Limit	Spent	Status	
2	Food	300	275	OK	
3	Rent	1000	1000	At Limit	
4	Travel	150	200	Over Budget	

D2 fx =IF(C2>B2, "Over Budget", IF(C2=B2, "At Limit", "OK"))

Summary of What You've Practiced:

Project	Functions Used
Grading System	IF, Nested IF, Conditional Formatting
Employee Lookup	INDEX, MATCH, Dynamic Lookup
Budget Alert	IF, AND, Conditional Formatting

VI. TROUBLESHOOTING AND TIPS

You've built some powerful tools with logical and lookup functions—but what happens when things don't work? This section is all about avoiding common mistakes, fixing errors, and writing cleaner, smarter formulas.

1. LOOKUP ERRORS & WHAT THEY MEAN

Here are the most common issues you'll face with functions like VLOOKUP, MATCH, or INDEX.

Error	What's Wrong?	How to Fix
#N/A	Lookup value not found	Double-check spelling or spacing. Use IFERROR() to handle
#REF!	You referenced a deleted row/column	Check your ranges. Rebuild the reference
#VALUE!	Incompatible value types	Make sure you're matching numbers to numbers or text to text
#NAME?	Misspelled function or missing quotes	Check spelling and use quotes for text inside formulas

2. BEST PRACTICES FOR LOOKUP FUNCTIONS

These pro tips will help you avoid 90% of lookup issues:

- Lock Your Ranges with $: When copying a lookup formula across rows or columns, ranges can shift and break. Use absolute references like this: =VLOOKUP(A2, $D$2:$F$100, 2, FALSE).
- Use Named Ranges for Clarity: Go to Data > Named ranges and name your lookup table "EmployeeList". Then write: =VLOOKUP(A2, EmployeeList, 2, FALSE). It's easier to read and manage later.
- Always Use FALSE in VLOOKUP: Unless your data is perfectly sorted in alphabetical or numerical order, always use the 4th argument as FALSE for exact match.

3. USE IFERROR() TO CLEAN UP YOUR FORMULAS

Instead of displaying ugly error messages to your readers, wrap your formula in IFERROR().

Example:

=IFERROR(VLOOKUP(A2, EmployeeList, 2, FALSE), "Not Found")

This will show "Not Found" instead of #N/A when the lookup fails.

You can also return a blank:

=IFERROR(formula, "")

Tip: Great for dashboards where a clean, polished look matters.

4. WHEN TO USE WHICH LOOKUP FUNCTION

Here's a cheat sheet to help you choose the right tool:

Function	Best When...
VLOOKUP	Simple, vertical lookups with key in 1st column
HLOOKUP	Same as above but horizontally
INDEX + MATCH	You need more flexibility (leftward lookups, speed)
LOOKUP	Data is sorted and you want a nearest match
INDIRECT	You want to reference other sheets dynamically
ADDRESS	You're building cell references from row/column numbers

Tips:

- Use test data when building complex logic formulas.
- Comment cells or nearby columns to explain what your formula does.
- Split long formulas into helper columns for clarity.
- Avoid merged cells in lookup ranges—they confuse formulas.
- Use Data Validation drop-downs to avoid typos in lookup keys.

Chapter 5: Text, Date, and Data Functions

I. TEXT FUNCTIONS

Google Sheets isn't just about numbers—it's also great at working with text. Whether you're cleaning up names, splitting data, combining columns, or formatting labels, text functions make it easy to structure and control words in your spreadsheet.

1. Why Use Text Functions?

Text functions help you: Clean up messy data (like names in all caps or with extra spaces); extract parts of a string (like the first name from a full name); combine multiple values into one; automate the creation of email addresses, usernames, or IDs; split data stored in a single column into several usable columns.

2. CONCATENATE and TEXTJOIN – Combining Text

i. CONCATENATE

Joins two or more pieces of text into one.

Syntax:

=CONCATENATE(text1, text2, ...)

Example:

=CONCATENATE(A2, " ", B2)

If A2 = "Taylor" and B2 = "Swift", this returns "Taylor Swift".

Use Case: Create full names, addresses, or custom labels.

ii. TEXTJOIN

Similar to CONCATENATE, but with a delimiter and the option to skip blanks.

Syntax:

=TEXTJOIN(delimiter, ignore_empty, text1, text2, ...)

Example:

=TEXTJOIN(" ", TRUE, A2, B2, C2)

If A2 = "Taylor", B2 = "", C2 = "Swift" → returns "Taylor Swift" (blanks are ignored!)

Tip: Use TEXTJOIN when working with many columns or optional values.

3. SPLIT – Break One Cell Into Many

Need to divide full names, separate tags, or clean up CSV-style entries? SPLIT is your best friend.

Syntax:

=SPLIT(text, delimiter)

Example:

=SPLIT(A2, ",")

If A2 = "Red,Green,Blue" → splits into "Red" | "Green" | "Blue".

4. SPLIT Auto-Detect (2025–2026 Update)

When you paste data into a cell — for example, "Red,Green,Blue" — Google Sheets can now automatically detect the delimiter and suggest splitting it into separate columns.

You'll see a popup offering:

- Auto-split.
- Choose delimiter.
- Ignore.

This behavior is powered by Smart Cleanup and saves time when importing CSV-style text.

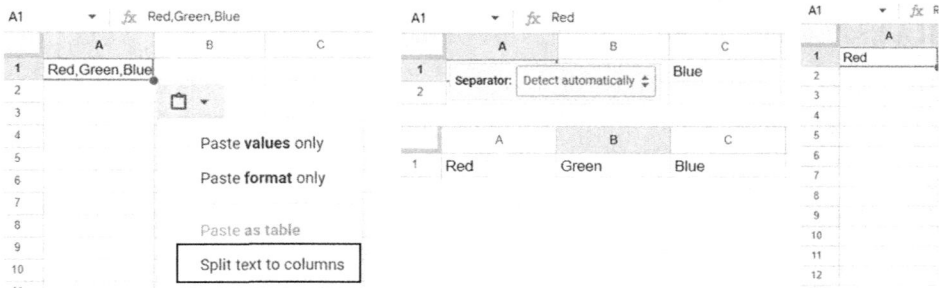

5. LEFT, RIGHT, MID – Extracting Parts of Text

Use these functions when you want to pluck part of a string based on character position.

Function	Purpose
LEFT(text, num_chars)	Gets characters from the beginning
RIGHT(text, num_chars)	Gets characters from the end
MID(text, start, num_chars)	Gets characters from the middle

Examples:

=LEFT("AB123", 2) → "AB"

=RIGHT("AB123", 3) → "123"

=MID("AB123", 3, 2) → "12"

Use Case: Extract codes, ID numbers, or standardize formatting.

6. LEN AND TRIM – COUNT AND CLEAN

i. *LEN(text)*

Returns the number of characters in a cell (including spaces).

Syntax:

=LEN("Google Sheets") → 13.

Use Case: Check for long text, set limits, or debug strange spacing.

ii. *TRIM(text)*

Removes extra spaces from the beginning and end of a string.

Syntax:

=TRIM(" Too   many spaces   ") → "Too many spaces".

Use Case: Clean up imported data, copy/paste text, or remove formatting issues.

Practice Example Table:

A (First Name)	B (Last Name)	C (Email)	D (Output Formula)
John	Doe	johndoe@gmail.com	=CONCATENATE(A2, " ", B2)
Jane	Smith	janesmith@example.com	=LEFT(C2, FIND("@", C2) - 1)

Result:

	A	B	C	D
1	**First Name**	**Last Name**	**Email**	**Output Formula**
2	John	Doe	johndoe@gmail.com	John Doe
3	Jane	Smith	janesmith@example.com	johndoe

SUMMARY OF KEY TEXT FUNCTIONS:

Function	What It Does
CONCATENATE	Joins text without skipping blanks
TEXTJOIN	Joins text with a delimiter, skips blanks
SPLIT	Splits text into multiple columns
LEFT/RIGHT	Extracts characters from beginning/end
MID	Extracts text from a middle position
LEN	Counts the number of characters
TRIM	Removes extra spaces

II. DATE AND TIME FUNCTIONS

Dates and times are a huge part of how we use spreadsheets—whether it's for tracking deadlines, calculating due dates, or measuring how long something took. Google Sheets makes it surprisingly easy to work with time, once you know the tools.

Let's break it down into clear, real-world examples.

1. HOW GOOGLE SHEETS STORES DATES (AND WHY IT MATTERS)

Google Sheets stores every date as a serial number, starting with 1 = January 1, 1900.

- **April 6, 2025** is stored as **45,768**.
- The number increases by **1** for each day.
- Time is stored as a decimal:
  » 0.5 = 12:00 PM (noon)
  » 0.25 = 6:00 AM

This is why you can do math with dates (like subtracting two dates to get the number of days between them).

2. TODAY() AND NOW()

These are your go-to functions for the current date and time:

Function	What It Returns
=TODAY()	The current date only (e.g., 4/6/2025)
=NOW()	The current date and time (e.g., 4/6/2025 1:34 PM)

Use Cases: Countdown to events; age or tenure calculations; auto-updating reports.

Example:

=TODAY() - A2

→ Calculates the number of days since the date in A2.

3. DATE Function – Building Dates from Parts

The DATE() function lets you construct a date using year, month, and day numbers.

Syntax:

=DATE(year, month, day)

Example:

=DATE(2025, 4, 6)

→ returns April 6, 2025.

Use Case: Combine separate columns like Year (2025), Month (4), Day (6) into a single usable date: =DATE(A2, B2, C2).

4. TEXT Function – Formatting Dates for Display

Sometimes you want to turn a date into text—maybe for a label, a header, or a cleaner layout.

Syntax:

=TEXT(date, "format")

Examples:

=TEXT(TODAY(), "MMMM D, YYYY")

→ April 6, 2025.

=TEXT(A2, "DD-MM-YYYY")

→ 06-04-2025.

Use Case: Create custom headers like "Report as of April 6, 2025":

=″Report as of " & TEXT(TODAY(), "MMMM D, YYYY")

	A	B	C
1	Report as of April 29, 2025		

5. DATEDIF AND NETWORKDAYS – DATE MATH

i. DATEDIF(start_date, end_date, unit)

Calculates the difference between two dates.

Unit	Returns
"D"	Number of days
"M"	Number of months
"Y"	Number of years

Example:

=DATEDIF(A2, TODAY(), "D")

→ returns how many days have passed since the date in A2.

	A	B	C
1	Start Date	End Date	Days Between
2	1/1/2025	1/10/2025	9

ii. NETWORKDAYS(start_date, end_date)

Returns the number of working days (excludes weekends, optionally holidays).

Example:

=NETWORKDAYS(A2, B2)

→ returns the number of weekdays between two dates.

	A	B	C
1	Start Date	End Date	Working Days
2	1/1/2025	1/10/2025	8

Use Case: Track work deadlines, project timelines, or vacation approvals.

iii. WORKDAY.INTL(start_date, num_days, [weekend], [holidays])

Returns a future or past workday based on a start date, number of days, custom weekends, and optional holidays.

Example:

=WORKDAY.INTL(DATE(2025,11,1),10,"0000011", {DATE(2025,11,11),DATE(2025,11,25)})

→ returns the date 10 workdays after Nov 1, 2025, treating Saturday and Sunday as weekends and skipping the listed holidays.

Use Case: Plan project timelines, schedule HR tasks, or manage work schedules across regions.

	A	B	C	D	E
1	11/17/2025				
2					

iv. NETWORKDAYS.INTL(start_date, end_date, [weekend], [holidays])

Returns the number of working days between two dates, excluding weekends and optional holidays.

Example:

=NETWORKDAYS.INTL(A2, B2, "0000011", {DATE(2025,11,25)})

→ returns the number of weekdays between two dates, considering custom weekends and holidays.

Use Case: Track work deadlines, calculate payroll periods, or manage vacation approvals.

	A	B	C	D	E
1	11/15/2025	11/30/2025			
2					
3	9				

SUMMARY OF KEY DATE FUNCTIONS:

Function	What It Does
TODAY()	Returns the current date

Function	What It Does
NOW()	Returns current date and time
DATE()	Builds a date from year, month, day
TEXT()	Formats a date as readable text
DATEDIF()	Calculates date differences (days, months, years)
NETWORKDAYS()	Returns number of business days between two dates
WORKDAY.INTL()	Returns a future or past workday based on a start date, number of days, custom weekends, and optional holidays
NETWORKDAYS.INTL()	Returns the number of working days between two dates, excluding custom weekends and optional holidays

You've now got the tools to handle anything time-related—deadlines, countdowns, age tracking, or custom-formatted reports.

III. DATA TRANSFORMATION AND FILTERING FUNCTIONS

Sometimes you want to filter, sort, or summarize your data without changing the original table. Google Sheets offers powerful functions that can dynamically reshape your data with just one formula.

Let's explore the game-changers: FILTER, UNIQUE, SORT, and how to use them together.

1. FILTER – SHOW ONLY WHAT YOU NEED

The FILTER function returns only the rows that match a condition.

Syntax:

=FILTER(range, condition)

Example:

Product	Sales
Apple	120
Banana	80
Grape	140

=FILTER(A2:B4, B2:B4 > 100)

Output: Only rows where Sales > 100 → Apple and Grape.

	A	B
1	Product	Sales
2	Apple	120
3	Banana	80
4	Grape	140
7	List of products with sales greater than 100	
8	Product	Sales
9	Apple	120
10	Grape	140

Cell A9: `=FILTER(A2:B4, B2:B4 > 100)`

Use Case: Show only **high performers;** filter data by **category**, **date**, or **status**.

2. UNIQUE – REMOVE DUPLICATES INSTANTLY

The UNIQUE function pulls only the distinct values from a list.

Syntax: =UNIQUE(range)

Example:

Category
Food
Travel
Food
Utilities

=UNIQUE(A2:A5)

Output:

	A	B
1	Category	Category
2	Food	Food
3	Travel	Travel
4	Food	Utilities
5	Utilities	

Cell B2: `=UNIQUE(A2:A5)`

Use Case:

- Create drop-down options.
- Summarize customer or product categories.
- Clean up messy imported data.

3. SORT – Organize Your Data Dynamically

The SORT function reorders your data without touching the original.

Syntax:

=SORT(range, sort_column, is_ascending)

Example:

Name	Score
Leo	88
Ava	95
Mia	80

=SORT(A2:B4, 2, FALSE)

Output: Sorted by Score, highest to lowest.

=SORT(A2:B4, 2, TRUE)

Output: Sorted by Score, lowest to highest.

4. Combine for Maximum Power

You can combine these functions to create live views of your data:

=SORT(FILTER(A2:B7, B2:B7>100), 2, FALSE)

→ Filters sales over 100 and sorts them in descending order.

	A	B	C	D
1	Name	Sales	Name	Sales
2	Alice	120	Diana	200
3	Bob	95	Alice	150
4	Alice	150	Bob	130
5	Charlie	80	Alice	120
6	Diana	200		
7	Bob	130		

=SORT(UNIQUE(A2:A7), 1, TRUE)

→ Alphabetical list of unique items.

	A	B	C
1	Name	Sales	Name
2	Alice	120	Alice
3	Bob	95	Bob
4	Alice	150	Charlie
5	Charlie	80	Diana
6	Diana	200	
7	Bob	130	

SUMMARY OF KEY DATA FUNCTIONS:

Function	What It Does
FILTER()	Shows rows that meet specific conditions
UNIQUE()	Removes duplicates from a list
SORT()	Reorders data dynamically

IV. INTRODUCTION TO ARRAYFORMULA

Have you ever wished you could apply a formula to an entire column without dragging it down? That's exactly what ARRAYFORMULA does—it lets you write one formula that automatically applies to multiple rows. Think of it as turning your formula into a smart auto-fill machine.

1. WHAT IS ARRAYFORMULA?

ARRAYFORMULA expands a formula to process an entire range of cells at once—no copying or dragging needed.

Syntax:

=ARRAYFORMULA(expression)

The expression often includes ranges instead of individual cells.

Example: Multiply Two Columns

Qty	Price	Total
2	5	

Qty	Price	Total
3	4	
1	10	

Without ARRAYFORMULA, you'd type in each row:

=A2*B2

But with ARRAYFORMULA, just do this once in cell C2:

=ARRAYFORMULA(A2:A4 * B2:B4)

Result: Fills all Total values in one go.

	A	B	C
1	Qty	Price	Total
2	2	5	10
3	3	4	12
4	1	10	10

2. COMMON USE CASES

i. Combine Columns:

=ARRAYFORMULA(A2:A & " " & B2:B)

→ Joins First and Last Names.

ii. Add Conditional Logic:

=ARRAYFORMULA(IF(C2:C = "", "", IF(C2:C >= 70, "Pass", "Fail")))

→ Assigns "Pass" or "Fail" only if there's a score entered.

iii. Date Calculations:

=ARRAYFORMULA(TODAY() - A2:A)

→ Calculates how many days ago each date in column A occurred.

Tip: Works great for project timelines, task due dates, or customer registration ages.

3. BEST PRACTICES WITH ARRAYFORMULA

Tip	Why It Matters
Avoid blank rows below	Otherwise, your sheet might fill thousands of rows!
Use helper columns	Break complex logic into separate steps
Use IFs to filter blank rows	Prevents junk values or errors from showing
Test on small data first	Easier to debug if something goes wrong

Example: Combine IF + ARRAYFORMULA

Let's say you want to check if a task is overdue:

Due Date	Status
4/15/2025	
4/29/2025	
5/13/2025	

Formula:

=ARRAYFORMULA(IF(A2:A="", "", IF(A2:A < TODAY(), "Overdue", "On Time")))

→ Evaluates each due date automatically and returns the appropriate status.

	A	B	C	D
	Due Date	Status		
2	4/15/2025	Overdue		
3	4/29/2025	On Time		
4	5/13/2025	On Time		

4. SUMMARY

Use Case	Example Formula
Multiply columns	=ARRAYFORMULA(A2:A * B2:B)
Combine text columns	=ARRAYFORMULA(A2:A & " " & B2:B)
Apply logic to full columns	=ARRAYFORMULA(IF(...))

You now have the skills to scale your formulas like a pro, automate repetitive logic, and reduce manual effort drastically.

V. QUERY FUNCTION ESSENTIALS

The QUERY function is like giving your spreadsheet a brain. It lets you write SQL-style commands (Structured Query Language) to:

- Filter rows, sort columns, group and summarize data.
- And do all of it without touching the original dataset.

1. BASIC QUERY()

Syntax:

=QUERY(data_range, "QUERY STRING", [header])

- data_range: Your table or dataset.
- "QUERY STRING": A text command (e.g., "SELECT A, B WHERE B > 100").
- header: Optional—use 1 if your data has headers.

Simple Example:

Name	Sales
Ava	150
Leo	80
Mia	200

=QUERY(A1:B4, "SELECT A, B WHERE B > 100", 1)

Output: Shows only Ava and Mia, whose sales are above 100.

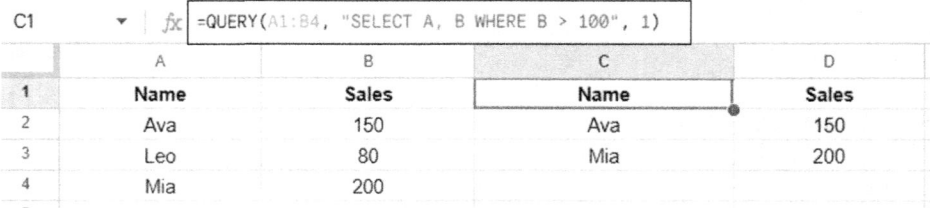

2. KEY CLAUSES IN THE QUERY LANGUAGE

Here are some of the most important parts of a query string:

Clause	What It Does	Example
SELECT	Picks columns to show	"SELECT A, B"
WHERE	Filters rows	"WHERE B > 100"

Clause	What It Does	Example
ORDER BY	Sorts results	"ORDER BY B DESC"
LIMIT	Restricts number of rows shown	"LIMIT 5"
LABEL	Renames columns in the result	"LABEL B 'Revenue'"
GROUP BY	Summarizes data by category	"GROUP BY A"
SUM(), AVG()	Aggregates values	"SELECT A, SUM(B) GROUP BY A"

3. Real-Life QUERY Examples

i. Show all sales above $500:

=QUERY(A1:B100, "SELECT A, B WHERE B > 500", 1)

ii. Sort employee scores descending:

=QUERY(A1:C100, "SELECT A, C ORDER BY C DESC", 1)

iii. Group expenses by category and total them:

=QUERY(A1:B100, "SELECT A, SUM(B) GROUP BY A", 1)

4. Bonus: Combine with Drop-downs

You can make your QUERY results dynamic by referencing a cell with a drop-down filter.

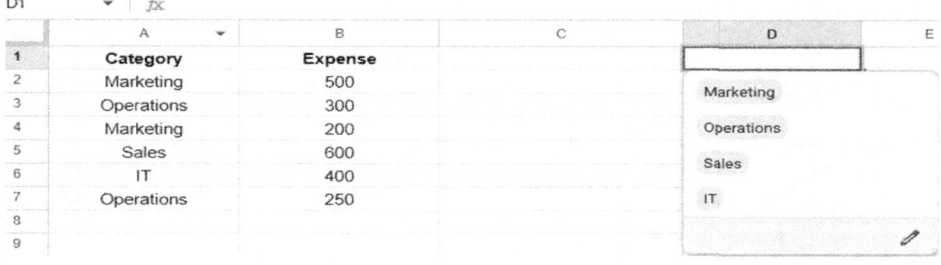

Example with category filter in D1:

=QUERY(A1:B7, "SELECT A, B WHERE A = '" & D1 & "'", 1)

	A	B	C	D	E
1	Category	Expense			
2	Marketing	500		Category	Expense
3	Operations	300			
4	Marketing	200			
5	Sales	600			
6	IT	400			
7	Operations	250			

Now when you select "Marketing" in D1, the table updates to only show Marketing rows!

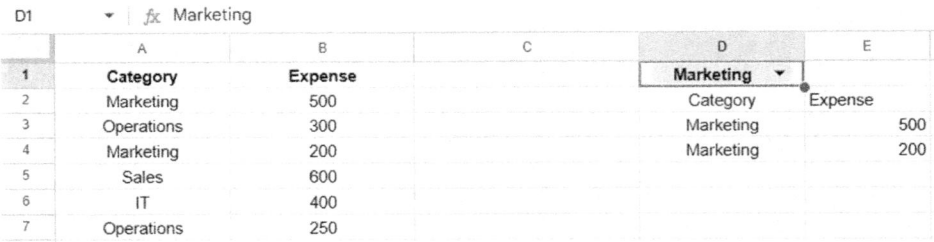

VI. PRACTICE PROJECTS

These mini-projects reinforce everything you've learned in this chapter and show how functions like TEXTJOIN, TODAY, ARRAYFORMULA, and QUERY work together in the wild.

1. PROJECT 1: CLEAN UP CONTACT INFO

You've imported contact info and it's all over the place. You need to combine first and last names, clean extra spaces, and create emails.

Sample Data:

A (First Name)	B (Last Name)	C (Domain)	D (Full Name)	E (Email Address)
John	Doe	example.com		
Ava	Smith	mysite.org		

Formulas:

- Full Name (D2): =ARRAYFORMULA(TRIM(A2:A & " " & B2:B))

Results:

	A	B	C	D	E
1	First Name	Last Name	Domain	Full Name	Email Address
2	John	Doe	example.com	JohnDoe	
3	Ava	Smith	mysite.org	AvaSmith	

D2: `=ARRAYFORMULA(TRIM(A2:A & " " & B2:B))`

- Email Address (E2):

=ARRAYFORMULA(LOWER(A2:A & "." & B2:B & "@" & C2:C))

Results:

	A	B	C	D	E
1	First Name	Last Name	Domain	Full Name	Email Address
2	John	Doe	example.com	JohnDoe	john.doe@example.com
3	Ava	Smith	mysite.org	AvaSmith	ava.smith@mysite.org

2. Project 2: Calculate Days Left Until Project Deadline

You want to know how many days are left until deadlines—and flag tasks that are overdue.

Sample Data:

A (Task)	B (Due Date)	C (Days Left)	D (Status)
Build report	5/10/2025		
Submit form	5/3/2025		

Formulas:

- Days Left (C2):

=ARRAYFORMULA(IF(B2:B="", "", B2:B - TODAY()))

	A	B	C	D
1	Task	Due Date	Days Left	Status
2	Build report	5/10/2025	11	
3	Submit form	4/28/2025	-1	

- Status (D2):

	A	B	C	D	E	F
				fx =ARRAYFORMULA(IF(B2:B = "", "", IF(B2:B < TODAY(), "Overdue", "On Track")))		
1	Task	Due Date	Days Left	Status		
2	Build report	5/10/2025	11	On Track		
3	Submit form	4/28/2025	-1	Overdue		

=ARRAYFORMULA(IF(B2:B="", "", IF(B2:B < TODAY(), "Overdue", "On Track")))

Bonus: Use conditional formatting to highlight Overdue rows in red and On Track rows in green.

3. PROJECT 3: CREATE A FILTERED SALES REPORT

You want a clean report showing only high-value sales, sorted from highest to lowest—without touching your original data.

Sample Data:

A (Product)	B (Region)	C (Sales)
Laptop	West	1200
Phone	East	600
Tablet	West	300

Formula:

In another part of your sheet:

=QUERY(A1:C4, "SELECT A, B, C WHERE C > 500 ORDER BY C DESC", 1)

Result:

	A	B	C	D	E	F
D1			fx =QUERY(A1:C4, "SELECT A, B, C WHERE C > 500 ORDER BY C DESC", 1)			
1	Product	Region	Sales	Product	Region	Sales
2	Laptop	West	1200	Laptop	West	1200
3	Phone	East	600	Phone	East	600
4	Tablet	West	300			

VII. TIPS AND BEST PRACTICES

Working with text, dates, and data transformations can get messy without the right habits. This section is all about the little things that make a big difference—whether you're debugging a complex formula, trying to speed up a slow sheet, or handing it off to a teammate.

1. WATCH FOR DATA TYPES

One of the most common reasons formulas break is mismatched data types.

Function	Problem	Fix
LEN(A2)	Returns 0 for a cell that looks filled	The value might be a number or empty string, not text
DATEDIF(A2,B2,"D")	Throws error or wrong result	Make sure both cells are actual dates, not text

Use These Helpers:

- =ISTEXT(A2) → Is this a text value?
- =ISNUMBER(A2) → Is this a number or date?
- =ISDATE(A2) → Not built-in! But you can check:

=IF(A2+0=A2, "Valid Date", "Not a Date")

Tip: Format your columns explicitly as text, date, or number to avoid silent errors.

2. NESTING FUNCTIONS SMARTLY

Nesting is when you put one function inside another—it's powerful but can get confusing fast. Make it easier to manage:

Start Simple:

=TEXT(DATE(2025, 4, 6), "MMMM D, YYYY")

Combine for Magic:

=ARRAYFORMULA(IF(A2:A="", "", "Due in " & (B2:B - TODAY()) & " days"))

This creates a full sentence like "Due in 3 days" for each task!

Tip: Break complex formulas into helper columns first, then combine them once you're sure it works.

3. When to Use Formulas vs Manual Cleanup

Just because you can write a formula, doesn't always mean you should.

Do It Manually When...	Use a Formula When...
You only need it once	You'll be updating or adding data often
It's a tiny dataset	The sheet is shared or live
You're correcting a typo	You're building a system or dashboard

Rule of Thumb:

If you'll do it more than once, use a formula.

Best Practices You Should Remember:

Tip	Why It Matters
Format columns explicitly	Prevents hidden errors and weird output
Use helper columns when nesting	Makes debugging easier
Always test on a small sample	Avoids large-scale formula chaos
Use IFERROR() for user-friendly output	Prevents ugly #VALUE! or #N/A displays
Label your formula cells or use comments	Helps collaborators understand your logic

4. Text + Regex Functions Are Now Recommended

Google Sheets now shows REGEXMATCH, REGEXEXTRACT, and REGEXREPLACE more prominently in suggestions because they are more powerful than basic text functions.

Use them when:

- Splitting unpredictable text.
- Extracting patterns.
- Cleaning imported data.
- Working with IDs or codes.

i. REGEXEXTRACT(text, regular_expression)

Extracts a portion of text matching a specified pattern.

Example:

=REGEXEXTRACT(A2,"[A-Z]{3}-\d+")

→ extracts a pattern like "ABC-12345" from the text in cell A2.

A2	▼	ƒx =REGEXEXTRACT(A1, "[A-Z]{3}-\d+")	
	A	▼	B
1	Order code: ABC-12345 received		
2	ABC-12345		

Use Case: Extract IDs, codes, or structured data from messy text.

ii. REGEXMATCH(text, regular_expression)

Returns TRUE if the text matches the specified pattern.

Example:

=REGEXMATCH(A2,"^\d{4}-\d{2}-\d{2}$")

→ returns TRUE if A2 contains a date in the format YYYY-MM-DD.

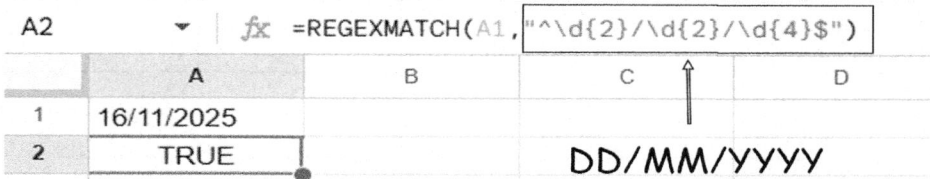

Use Case: Validate text patterns, check input formats, or flag data errors.

iii. REGEXREPLACE(text, regular_expression, replacement)

Replaces parts of text matching a pattern with a new value.

Example:

=REGEXREPLACE(A2,"[^\d]","")

→ removes all non-digit characters from the text in A2.

	A	B
	A2 ▼ ƒx =REGEXREPLACE(A1,"[^\d]","")	
1	Order #ABC-12345!	
2	12345	

Use Case: Clean imported data, remove unwanted characters, or standardize codes.

REGEX Quick Reference Table:

Pattern	Meaning	Example
^	Start of string	^Hello
$	End of string	world$
.	Any single character	c.t → cat/cot/cut
*	0+ times	a*
+	1+ times	a+
?	Optional (0 or 1)	colou?r
{n}	Exactly n	a{3}
{n,}	At least n	a{2,}
{n,m}	Between n–m	a{2,5}
[abc]	One of a, b, c	—
[^abc]	Not a, b, or c	—
[0-9]	Digit range	—
[A-Za-z]	Letter range	—
\d	Digit	\d+
\D	Non-digit	—
\w	Word char	—
\W	Non-word	—
\s	Whitespace	—

94

Pattern	Meaning	Example
\S	Non-whitespace	—
(abc)	Group	(cat)+
(?:abc)	Non-capturing	—
cat|dog	OR	—
\.	Literal dot	a\.b
\\	Literal backslash	—
\d+	Extract numbers	REGEXEXTRACT("A123","\d+")
[A-Za-z]+	Extract letters	—
[^0-9]	Remove non-numeric	REGEXREPLACE(A1,"[^0-9]","")
[\w.-]+@[\w.-]+\.\w+	Email pattern	—

Chapter 6: Charts, Graphs & Dashboards

I. WHY VISUALIZATION MATTERS

Data visualizations: Help you spot patterns and trends instantly; make your work look professional and polished; turn raw data into insights; are easier to present and understand—especially for non-data people.

Use a Chart when you want to: Compare sales by product; see trends over time; show proportions or parts of a whole.

Use a Dashboard when you want to: Create a one-page summary of multiple data sources; add interactive elements (like drop-downs); build something presentation-ready or for real-time monitoring.

II. CHOOSING THE RIGHT CHART

1. Chart Types and When to Use Them

Google Sheets offers many chart types—but here are the most useful ones you'll actually use, and why you'd pick each one.

i. Column / Bar Chart

Best for: Comparing categories.

Use it for: Product sales by category; survey results; monthly expenses by type.

Tip: Use bar charts for long category names; use column charts for time-based data (e.g., Jan–Feb–Mar).

ii. Line Chart

Best for: Showing trends over time.

Use it for: Sales over 12 months; website traffic by week; weight tracking over time.

Tip: Great for showing progress, growth, or seasonality.

iii. Pie Chart

Best for: Showing parts of a whole.

Use it for: Expense breakdown; market share; survey responses (e.g., favorite color).

Tip: Keep it to 5 slices or fewer—more than that gets messy.

iv. Combo Chart

Best for: Comparing two data types (e.g., sales vs profit margin).

Use it for: Revenue vs target; orders vs return rate; grades vs attendance.

Tip: Combo charts let you combine a bar and a line, and they support a second Y-axis if your data types need separate scales.

v. Area Chart

Best for: Emphasizing volume over time.

Use it for: Cumulative revenue; stockpile of inventory; web traffic buildup.

vi. Scatter Chart

Best for: Spotting relationships between two variables.

Use it for: Height vs weight; study hours vs test scores; product price vs satisfaction.

vii. Other Helpful Chart Types

Google Sheets includes a few more chart types that are useful once you've mastered the basics:

- Map chart – visualizes data by geographic region to show distribution or intensity across locations.
- Histogram – groups numeric values into buckets to show distribution (great for exam scores or response times).
- Treemap – shows parts-of-a-whole using nested rectangles, useful when you have many categories.
- Waterfall – shows how a starting value increases/decreases step by step until it reaches a final total.
- Candlestick / OHLC – designed for stock or financial data.
- Table chart – turns your data into a sortable "chart table," often used in dashboards.
- Radar chart – compares multiple metrics on radial axes to reveal strengths, weaknesses, or performance profiles.
- Gauge chart – displays progress toward a goal using a dial-style indicator (great for KPIs or completion percentages).

- Scorecard – highlights a key metric with optional comparison to a previous period (ideal for dashboards).
- Organizational chart – shows hierarchical relationships using connected boxes (useful for company or team structures).
- Timeline chart – displays events or durations along a chronological axis (great for project schedules or historical sequences).

You don't need these for everyday work, but they're good tools to know about as your dashboards become more advanced.

2. REAL-LIFE USE CASES (CHART MATCHMAKER)

Scenario	Best Chart Type
Comparing monthly spending categories	Pie or Bar Chart
Tracking website visitors weekly	Line Chart
Showing sales vs profit on one chart	Combo Chart
Visualizing daily progress toward goal	Area Chart or Line
Analyzing price vs performance	Scatter Chart
Showing pass/fail rates by subject	Column Chart

Pro Tips for Chart Selection:

- Choose a chart that simplifies, not decorates.
- Always label your axes—make it clear what the viewer is seeing.
- Use colors intentionally (e.g., red for losses, green for gains).
- Don't overcomplicate—less is more.

III. CREATING A CHART IN GOOGLE SHEETS

1. SELECTING THE RIGHT DATA

Before anything else, your chart needs well-structured data. For example:

Month	Sales
Jan	1000
Feb	1200
Mar	900

Tips:

- Always include headers (they become axis labels or legends).

- Avoid blank rows or columns.
- Don't use merged cells—they confuse charts.

If you're unsure, select your data and try inserting a chart—Sheets will often auto-detect and do the right thing.

2. Using the Insert Chart Tool

Here's how to go from data to chart in just a few clicks:

1. Highlight your data table, including headers.
2. Go to the menu: Insert > Chart.
3. A default chart will appear (usually a column chart).
4. The Chart Editor panel appears on the right.

3. Editing and Customizing Charts

In the Chart Editor, you can do all kinds of awesome customizations:

i. Change Chart Type

- Click the Setup tab.
- Choose from bar, line, pie, scatter, etc.

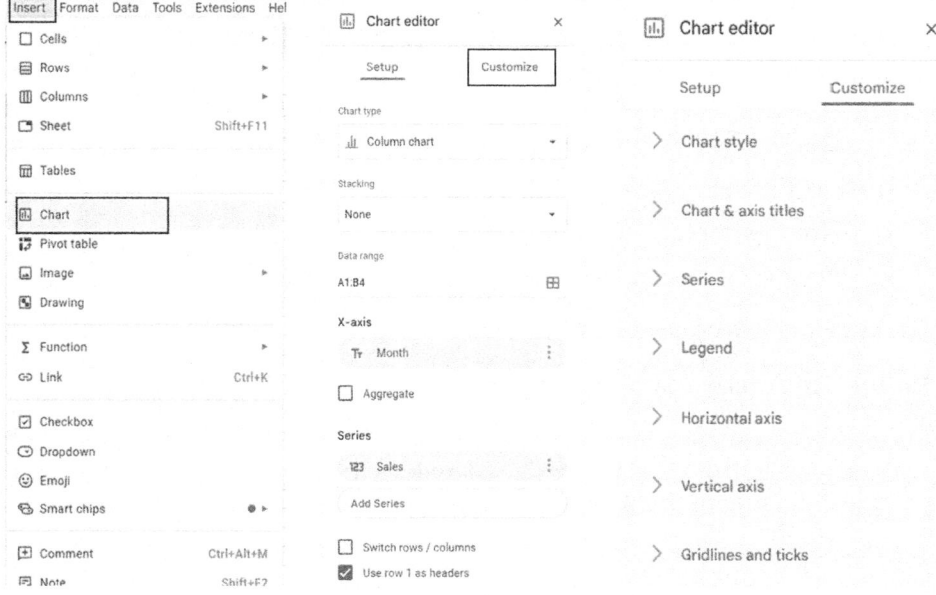

ii. Customize Appearance (under "Customize" tab):

Option	What It Does
Chart Style	Adjusts the overall look and feel—background color, border, font, and 3D effect
Chart & Axis Titles	Add or edit titles for the chart, horizontal axis, and vertical axis for clarity
Series	Customize each data series (color, line thickness, point style, bar shape, etc.)
Legend	Choose position (top, bottom, left, right, none) and customize font and size
Horizontal Axis	Customize font, format, scale, and appearance of the X-axis
Vertical Axis	Set min/max values, format numbers, add prefix/suffix, and adjust label style
Gridlines & Ticks	Show or hide gridlines and tick marks to improve chart readability
Data Labels	Display actual data values on bars, columns, points, or slices
Trendlines	Add a trendline or moving average to reveal patterns or projections

Example:

Want a pie chart that labels each slice with percentage?

- Select Chart type > Pie chart.
- Go to Customize > Pie chart.
- Turn on "Slice label" and choose "Percentage".

Looks clean. Reads easy. Wins points.

Bonus: Interactive Customization

Click directly on any element in the chart (title, bar, axis labels) and Sheets will let you: Edit it directly; resize or delete it; drag and move the legend; change colors from the paint bucket icon.

Quick Fixes for Common Chart Issues

Problem	Fix It By...
Wrong data showing	Check if you highlighted the right range
X and Y axis flipped	Switch row/column toggle in Chart Editor > Setup tab
Empty chart	Make sure data isn't all blank or merged
Bars not showing all labels	Expand the chart size or rotate labels (Customize tab)

IV. ADVANCED CHART FEATURES

Once you've mastered basic charting, it's time to dive into enhanced customization and interactivity. These features let you communicate more nuanced insights and make your charts dynamic and user-friendly.

1. CUSTOMIZING WITH SERIES AND DUAL AXES

Let's say you want to show sales and profit margin on one chart. These are different types of data—sales is a number, margin is a percentage. You can use the Combo Chart + Dual Axes.

1. Insert your chart as normal.
2. In Chart Editor, switch the Chart type to "Combo chart".
3. Go to Customize > Series.
4. Select one data series (e.g., "Profit Margin").
5. Check the box: "Axis: Right axis".

Now:

- Left Y-axis shows sales.
- Right Y-axis shows profit margin (%).

Example Table:

Month	Sales	Profit Margin
Jan	1000	0.25
Feb	1200	0.18
Mar	900	0.30

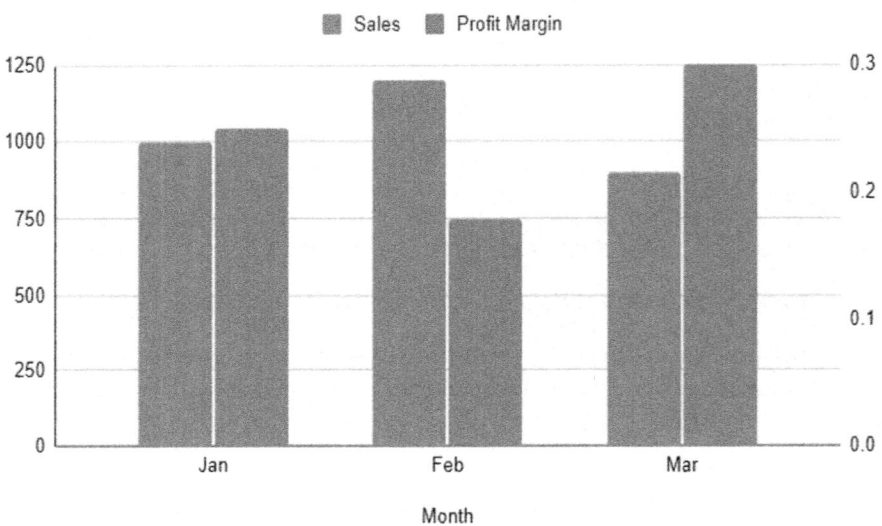

2. Dynamic Charts with Drop-Down Menus

Wouldn't it be cool if users could select a category from a drop-down and your chart updated automatically? You can do that—without macros—by combining: A drop-down list (via Data Validation); a filtered dataset (using FILTER or QUERY); a chart tied to that filtered data.

Steps:

1. Create a drop-down using Data > Data validation. Example: List of Regions in F1.
2. Use FILTER: =FILTER(A2:C, B2:B = F1).
3. Build a chart based on the filtered range.

Example Table:

Month	Region	Sales
Jan	North	1000

Month	Region	Sales
Feb	South	1200
Mar	Central	1500
Apr	North	1300
May	South	1400
Jun	Central	1600

Follow the steps above in order. Now when you choose "North" in the drop-down, the chart updates to only show North region data.

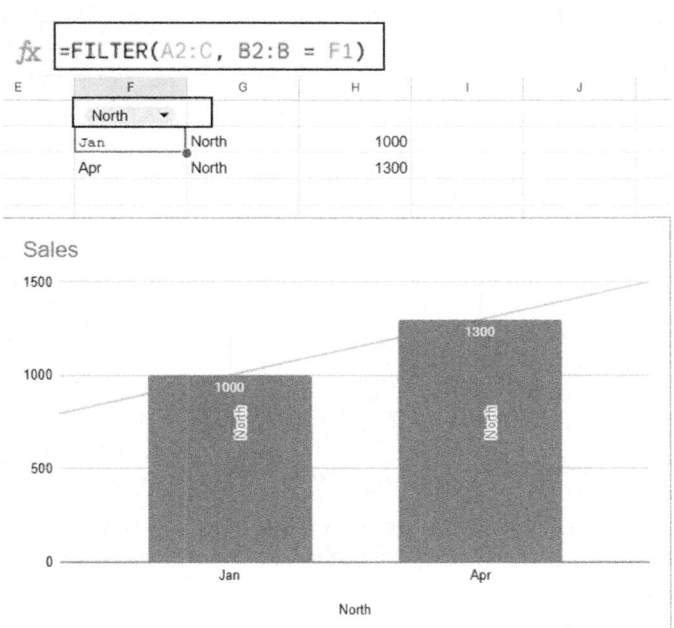

Smart Use Cases for Dynamic Charts:

Use Case	How It Works
Team progress tracker	Choose team member from a drop-down
Monthly sales breakdown	Filter data by month
Category spending analyzer	Show one category at a time
Real-time KPI monitoring	Tie charts to a live updating dataset

Tips for Polishing Advanced Charts:

Pro Tip	Why It Helps
Use transparent chart backgrounds	Cleaner integration in dashboards
Apply consistent color themes	Professional look and easier to read
Add trendlines (Customize > Series)	Instantly show direction or pattern over time
Turn on data labels	View exact values without hovering
Don't overcrowd your axes	Rotate text or adjust chart size to fit

Now your charts aren't just pretty—they're interactive, responsive, and tailored to your viewer.

V. BUILDING AN INTERACTIVE DASHBOARD

A dashboard is a visual summary of your key data—often on one clean, scroll-free screen. It allows you to quickly answer questions like:

- "How are we doing this month?"
- "Which product is performing best?"
- "What needs our attention right now?"

1. WHAT IS A DASHBOARD IN GOOGLE SHEETS?

It's not a separate tool—it's a smartly designed sheet that: Pulls data from other sheets (or tabs); displays it with charts and key metrics; uses interactivity (like drop-downs or slicers); is clean, focused, and print/presentation-ready.

Great dashboards are easy to read at a glance.

2. LAYOUT & DESIGN PRINCIPLES

Before you start throwing in charts, get your layout right.

General Structure:

Area	Contents
Header	Dashboard title, report period, filters
Left column	KPIs, scorecards, mini charts
Right column	Detailed charts, trend graphs
Bottom row	Tables, notes, or links to data sources

Tips for a Clean Design:

Principle	How to Apply It
Grid layout	Use cell blocks and align items neatly
White space	Add breathing room between charts and metrics
Color palette	Stick to 2–3 colors max for consistency
Clear labels	Every chart and number should say what it is
Avoid clutter	Don't show every column of raw data—summarize instead

3. ELEMENTS OF A SIMPLE DASHBOARD

Here's what a beginner-friendly Google Sheets dashboard might include:

Title/Report Period:

- Use cell values + formulas.
- Example: ="Sales Dashboard - " & TEXT(TODAY(), "MMMM YYYY").

KPI Tiles (aka Scorecards):

Eg: SaleData:

Product	Units Sold	Total Sales ($)
Sports T-Shirt	150	4,500
Running Shoes	80	6,000
Yoga Pants	120	5,400
Hoodie	90	4,050
Gym Bag	60	3,350

Metric	Formula
Total Sales	=SUM(SalesData!C2:C)
Top Product	=INDEX(A2:A, MATCH(MAX(B2:B), B2:B, 0))
Avg Order Value	=AVERAGE(SalesData!C2:C)

You can style these with: Large bold text; borders and fill color; conditional formatting to highlight goals.

Metric	Value	Formula (if using Google Sheets)
Total Sales	$24,300	=SUM(SalesData!C2:C)

Metric	Value	Formula (if using Google Sheets)
Top-Selling Product	Running Shoes	=INDEX(A2:A, MATCH(MAX(B2:B), B2:B, 0))
Average Order Value	$4,860	=AVERAGE(SalesData!C2:C)

Example of 3 KPI boxes:

B3   fx =INDEX(Data!A2:A, MATCH(MAX(Data!C2:C), Data!C2:C, 0))

	A	B
1	Sales Dashboard – April 2025	
2	Total Sales	24,300
3	Top-Selling Product	Running Shoes
4	Average Order Value	4,860

Charts & Trends:

Add bar, line, or combo charts showing: Monthly revenue; sales by product/category; conversion rates.

Filters:

- Use drop-downs or slicers (more in next section).
- Allow viewer to filter by region, month or product line.

EXAMPLE DASHBOARD LAYOUT (SIMPLE VIEW):

KPI Tiles	Charts
Total Sales: $24,300	📊 Bar: Sales by Product
Top Category: Apparel	📈 Line: Sales Trend Over Time
Conversion Rate: 4.8%	🥧 Pie: Traffic Sources

You're now well on your way to building your first polished dashboard—a skill that's useful for work, freelancing, personal planning, or side projects.

4. DASHBOARD THEMES

Google Sheets now includes preset dashboard themes.

These instantly apply coordinated colors to:

- Charts
- Headings

- Boxes and shapes.
- Borders and fills.

Themes help you keep your entire dashboard visually consistent without manually recoloring every chart.

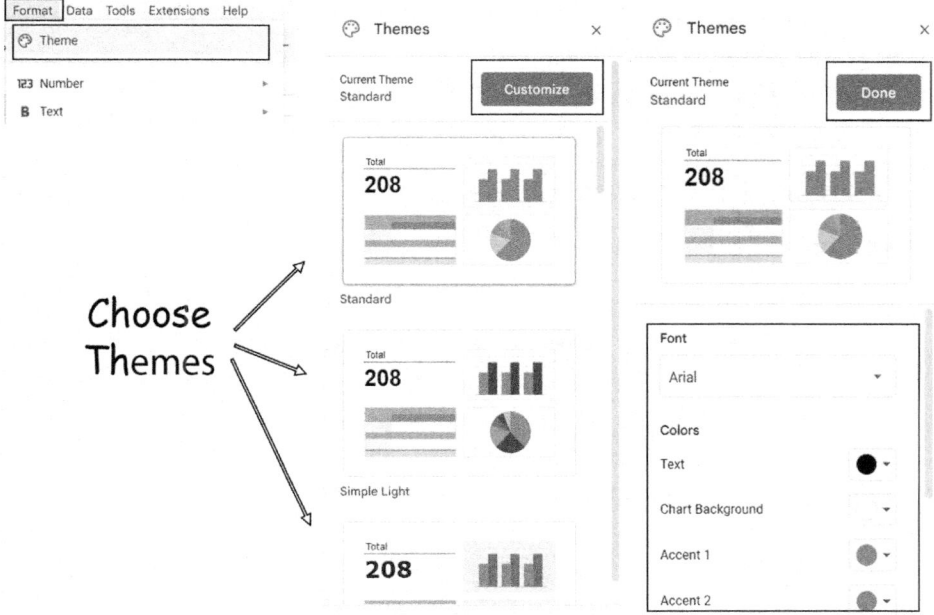

VI. USING SLICERS IN GOOGLE SHEETS

1. WHAT IS A SLICER?

A Slicer is a visual filter that lets users interact directly with your charts or pivot tables—without editing formulas or using drop-downs. Think of it like a filter button panel that: Updates charts in real time; looks clean and professional; is easy for anyone to use (no tech skills needed).

Slicers are perfect for dashboards, team reports, or client-facing sheets.

2. WHEN TO USE A SLICER

Use Case	Slicer Example
Filter sales by region	"East", "West", "Central" buttons
Show performance by team member	Filter by name
Display tasks by status	"To Do", "In Progress", "Done"
View KPIs by month	"Jan", "Feb", "Mar", etc.

3. **ADDING AND CONFIGURING A SLICER**

Let's walk through creating your first slicer:

1. Select your chart or pivot table.
2. Go to Data > Add a Slicer.
3. The slicer appears on the sheet—usually near the chart.
4. In the right panel:
   » Choose your data range.
   » Select the column to filter by (e.g., Region or Month).
5. Customize the style (title, font size, color).

Example:

	A	B
1	Region	Sales ($)
2	North	10,000
3	Central	8,000
4	South	12,000

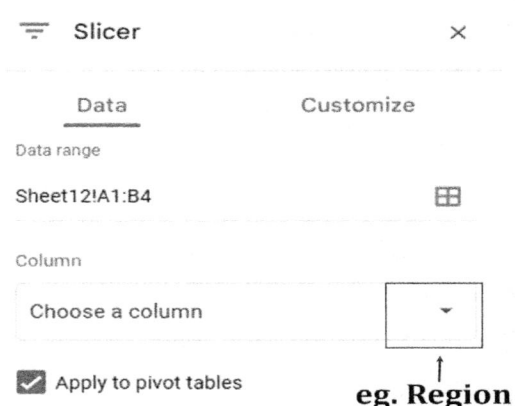

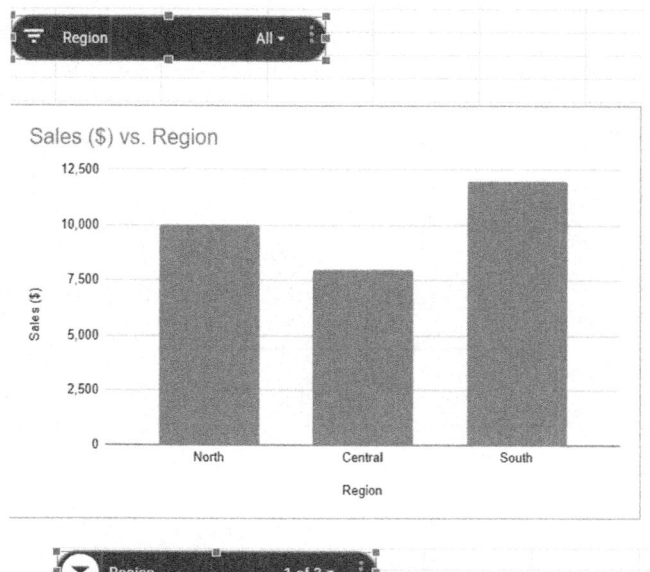

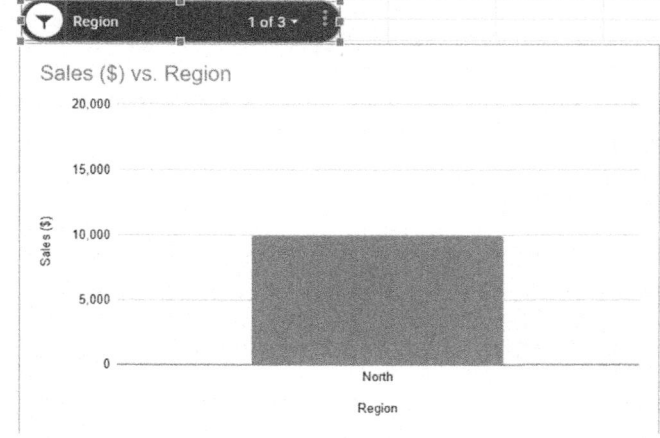

Pro Tip: Use Slicers with Pivot Tables:

Slicers work best with structured data, especially pivot tables. Create a pivot table first, then attach a slicer to it to filter live. You can even link multiple charts to the same slicer if they share the same dataset.

Slicer Settings to Explore:

Option	What It Does
Filter Type	Choose between single and multi-select
Title	Add a clear label like "Select Region"

Option	What It Does
Style	Change background, font, and borders
Position	Place slicers to the side of your dashboard

Good slicers are clear, compact, and easy to interact with.

Quick Troubleshooting:

Problem	How to Fix It
Slicer not filtering chart	Make sure slicer and chart share same dataset
Slicer filtering wrong field	Double-check the selected column
Data not updating	Try refreshing the slicer or reselecting range

VII. LINKING DATA ACROSS SHEETS FOR DASHBOARDS

1. PULLING DATA FROM OTHER TABS

Great dashboards don't mix raw data with visuals—they pull data from a "Data" tab and keep the dashboard clean.

Use this simple formula: =SheetName!CellReference

Example:

=SalesData!B2

→ This pulls the value from cell B2 in the tab named "SalesData"

Use this to: Pull totals; reference key categories; build a summary section on your dashboard tab.

2. CREATING DYNAMIC METRICS (KPI TILES)

KPI tiles are like digital scorecards—they highlight key numbers at the top of your dashboard.

Common Metrics:

Metric	Formula Example
Total Sales	=SUM(Data!C2:C)
Top-Selling Product	=INDEX(A2:A, MATCH(MAX(B2:B), B2:B, 0))
Orders This Month	=COUNTIF(Data!A2:A, ">=4/1/2025")
Average Order Value	=AVERAGE(Data!C2:C)

Wrap in formatting for visual pop: large font, bold numbers, fill color and borders.

3. CONDITIONAL FORMATTING FOR KPI TILES

To make metrics stand out, apply visual cues:

Example	Conditional Format
Sales over $10,000	Green background
Negative value or under budget	Red text
On-target percentage	Yellow fill for values between 90–100%

4. CREATING A "LIVE" DASHBOARD TAB

Now that you're linking cells, adding metrics, and using slicers—you've built a sheet that updates automatically as the underlying data changes.

A full setup looks like:

- Raw Data tab: where info is entered/imported.
- Calc tab (optional): where formulas prep the numbers.
- Dashboard tab: where visuals and KPIs live.
- Control tab (optional): for dropdowns or slicers.

Using separate tabs = clean structure, easy updates, scalable design.

VIII. PUBLISHING AND SHARING DASHBOARDS

Creating a beautiful dashboard is just one part of the job. The other? Making sure it's easy to share, safe to access, and clean to present. Let's walk through how to do it like a pro.

1. PREPARING FOR VIEWERS

Before sharing your dashboard with a teammate, boss, or client, run through this quick checklist:

☐ Hide raw data tabs (right-click tab > Hide).

☐ Lock formulas or ranges (so no one breaks them).

☐ Rename tabs clearly (e.g., "Dashboard", not "Sheet1").

☐ Test slicers and drop-downs to ensure they work as expected.

☐ Preview on different screen sizes if being shared widely.

Tip: Keep a copy of the original sheet before sharing, just in case someone edits something accidentally.

2. SHARING OPTIONS

Google Sheets gives you a few ways to share:

i. Direct Sharing

- Click the Share button (top right).
- Add email addresses.
- Choose permissions:
  » Viewer – see only.
  » Commenter – add comments.
  » Editor – full access (use with care!).

ii. Get a Shareable Link

- Click "Copy link".
- Set link access:
  » Anyone with the link.
  » Viewer / Commenter / Editor.

This is great for sharing in Slack, email, or newsletters.

3. PUBLISH TO WEB

Want to embed your dashboard into a website, Google Site, or blog? Here's how:

1. Go to File > Share > Publish to Web.
2. Choose the tab to publish (usually your Dashboard tab).
3. Copy the embed code or link.
4. Paste it into your website or Google Slides.

Note: Published versions are view-only and do not update instantly. Use for stable reports, not live metrics.

To unpublish, go to File → Share → Publish to web → Stop publishing.

4. PRINTING OR EXPORTING AS PDF

Want to turn your dashboard into a PDF report? Steps:

1. File > Print.

2. Set:
   - » Fit to page width.
   - » Landscape or Portrait (depends on layout). Margins = Narrow.
3. Use "Set print area" to highlight only the dashboard.

Pro Tips for Sharing Dashboards:

Situation	Best Option
One-time report or slide deck	Export to PDF or publish to web
Client portal or internal use	Share via link with Viewer access
Internal team with collaboration	Share with Editor or Commenter access + protect formulas
Website / presentation dashboard	Publish as embed or link

IX. PRACTICE PROJECTS – BUILD YOUR OWN DASHBOARDS

These projects are designed to give you: A template to follow; a chance to apply real functions; a feel for structuring a dashboard layout.

1. DASHBOARD PROJECT 1: EXPENSE TRACKER

Use Case: Track monthly personal or business spending and spot where your money goes.

Expense Tracker

Date	Category	Amount	Description	Month	Payment Method
2025-04-01	Groceries	120.50	Supermarket shopping	April	Credit Card
2025-04-02	Transport	45.00	Gas refill	April	Cash
2025-04-03	Entertainment	15.00	Movie ticket	April	Debit Card
2025-04-05	Dining Out	35.20	Lunch with friends	April	Credit Card
2025-04-07	Utilities	60.00	Electricity bill	April	Bank Transfer

Date	Category	Amount	Description	Month	Payment Method
2025-04-10	Groceries	98.70	Weekly grocery run	April	Credit Card
2025-04-12	Transport	12.00	Train ticket	April	Cash
2025-04-15	Shopping	85.00	New shoes	April	Credit Card
2025-04-18	Dining Out	42.00	Dinner at restaurant	April	Debit Card
2025-04-20	Miscellaneous	25.00	Gift for friend	April	Cash

Structure:

- Left column: KPI Tiles (Total Spent, Top Category, Remaining Budget eg 500).
- Right column: Pie chart of spending by category, line chart showing trend.

KPI	Formula Example (Google Sheets)
Total Spent	=SUM(C2:C11)
Top Category	=INDEX(B2:B11, MATCH(MAX(C2:C11), C2:C11, 0))
Remaining Budget (e.g. $500)	=500 - SUM(C2:C11)
Filtered View by Month	=FILTER(A2:F11, E2:E11 = "April")

Suggested Charts for Dashboard:

- Pie Chart: Spending by Category.
- Line Chart: Spending over time (based on Date).
- Bar Chart: Amount by Payment Method.

Key Elements:

- SUM() – for total expenses.
- MAX() + INDEX() – for top spending category.
- QUERY() or FILTER() – for drop-down-controlled breakdown.
- Pie chart by category.
- Line chart by month.

Interactive Elements:

- Drop-down to filter by Month.
- Conditional formatting on overspending.

2. Dashboard Project 2: Team Task Overview

Use Case: Track project progress and team contributions in a shared team environment.

Team Task Tracker:

Task ID	Task Name	Owner	Status	Due Date	Completion Date	Priority	Category
T001	Design Homepage	Alice	Done	2025-04-05	2025-04-03	High	Design
T002	Set Up Database	Bob	In Progress	2025-04-10		High	Development
T003	Write Copy	Carol	To Do	2025-04-12		Medium	Content
T004	QA Testing	Dave	To Do	2025-04-15		Medium	QA
T005	User Feedback Survey	Alice	Done	2025-04-07	2025-04-06	Low	Research
T006	Backend API Integration	Bob	In Progress	2025-04-14		High	Development
T007	Email Campaign	Carol	Done	2025-04-09	2025-04-08	Medium	Marketing
T008	Logo Redesign	Alice	In Progress	2025-04-13		Low	Design
T009	Security Audit	Dave	To Do	2025-04-18		High	QA
T010	Blog Article	Carol	Done	2025-04-11	2025-04-11	Low	Conten

Suggested KPI Metrics for Top Row:

KPI	Example Formula (Google Sheets)
Tasks Completed	=COUNTIF(D2:D11, "Done")
% Completed	=COUNTIF(D2:D11, "Done") / COUNTA(D2:D11)

KPI	Example Formula (Google Sheets)
Overdue Tasks	=COUNTIF(E2:E11, "<"&TODAY()) - COUNTIF(D2:D11, "Done")

Structure:

- Top row: KPIs (Tasks Completed, % Done, Overdue Count).
- Middle section: Bar chart (tasks by team member), stacked column (task status breakdown).
- Bottom: Filterable task list.

Key Elements:

- COUNTIF(), COUNTA() – for task counts.
- TODAY() + IF() – for overdue alerts.
- Stacked bar chart showing To Do / In Progress / Done.
- Slicer for team member selection.

Interactive Elements:

- Slicer: Filter tasks by team member.
- Checkbox columns (optional) for marking completion.

3. **DASHBOARD PROJECT 3: SALES BY REGION**

Use Case: Visualize performance across multiple regions or sales channels.

Regional Sales Data:

Date	Region	Salesperson	Product	Units Sold	Unit Price	Total Sales	Target	Channel
2025-04-01	East	Alice	Laptop	12	800	9600	8500	Online
2025-04-02	West	Bob	Headphones	30	50	1500	2000	Retail
2025-04-02	Central	Carol	Smartphone	18	600	10800	10000	Online
2025-04-03	East	Alice	Monitor	10	200	2000	2500	Retail
2025-04-04	West	Dave	Keyboard	25	40	1000	1200	Online
2025-04-05	Central	Carol	Laptop	8	800	6400	7000	Retail

Date	Region	Salesperson	Product	Units Sold	Unit Price	Total Sales	Target	Channel
2025-04-06	East	Alice	Smartphone	10	600	6000	5000	Online
2025-04-06	West	Bob	Mouse	35	20	700	800	Retail
2025-04-07	Central	Dave	Headphones	40	50	2000	2200	Online
2025-04-07	East	Alice	Keyboard	15	40	600	900	Retail

KPI Tiles (Suggested Metrics):

KPI Name	Sample Formula (Google Sheets)
Total Sales	=SUM(G2:G11)
Highest Region	=INDEX(B2:B11, MATCH(MAX(G2:G11), G2:G11, 0))
Monthly Growth (%)	Compare with previous month using dynamic formula logic

Structure:

- KPI Tiles: Total Sales, Highest Region, Monthly Growth %.
- Combo chart: Sales vs Target.
- Table: Top 5 Products.
- Filters: Region and Date.

Key Elements:

- QUERY() for filtered data.
- SORT(), LARGE(), INDEX() for top products.
- Combo chart: bar for sales, line for target.
- Pie chart or map-style breakdown by region (optional add-on).

Interactive Elements:

- Drop-downs for Region and Month.
- Dynamic chart using FILTER() based on drop-downs.

Tips for Building Your Own Dashboards:

Tip	Why It Matters
Sketch layout before building	Helps you organize better
Build formulas before charts	Ensures the data is clean and dynamic
Test slicers and filters early	Fix issues before final styling
Use consistent fonts and colors	Looks clean and professional
Label everything	Viewers shouldn't have to guess what it means

X. TIPS FOR BETTER VISUALS

Whether you're presenting to your boss, your team, or just yourself - a well-designed chart or dashboard should be clear, focused, and easy on the eyes. This section helps you avoid common mistakes and polish your visuals like a pro.

1. DOs – What to Aim For

√ What to Do	X Why It Works
Keep it simple	Removes clutter, makes key info pop
Use whitespace	Prevents visual overload
Highlight what matters	Use color or bold for totals, trends, warnings
Stick to 2–3 colors max	Keeps your dashboard consistent and readable
Label everything	Helps the reader understand at a glance
Align elements	Gives your layout structure and professionalism
Use consistent formats	E.g., all currency in $, all dates as "MMM YYYY"
Add context (headers/notes)	Explains what the user is seeing and why it matters

2. DON'Ts – Common Mistakes to Avoid

X Don't Do This	☺ Why It's a Problem
Use too many chart types	Confuses the viewer—stick to 1–2 per dashboard
Show raw data on dashboard tab	Makes layout messy—use links or references instead

✗ Don't Do This	☹ Why It's a Problem
Use 3D charts	Looks cool, but skews data and readability
Overuse colors or gradients	Distracting and hard to interpret
Merge too many cells	Breaks responsiveness and causes layout issues
Forget to test on other screens	Your design may break on smaller devices

3. Visual Clean-Up Checklist

Before publishing or presenting your dashboard, go through this quick visual audit:

☐ Fonts are consistent (no wild mix of styles/sizes).

☐ Chart axes and legends are clearly labeled.

☐ KPIs are bold and distinct.

☐ Filters/slicers are easy to find and intuitive.

☐ No excess gridlines, text, or duplicated info.

☐ Dashboard fits on one screen (or prints well).

4. Pro-Level Styling Tips

Trick	Result
Use light gray borders in tables	Creates separation without overwhelming the eye
Center-align KPIs	Focuses attention and improves symmetry
Conditional formatting bars	Create progress bars right in cells
Use shapes for section headers	E.g., colored rectangles with white bold text
Add a hoverable help column	Insert notes or instructions using the comment tool

Chapter 7: Automation with Google Sheets

I. Why Automate in Google Sheets?

1. Benefits of Automation

- Save time: No more manual copy-pasting or data entry.
- Increase accuracy: Eliminate human error from repetitive tasks.
- Improve efficiency: Run reports and updates faster.
- Scale easily: Manage more data, more people, more projects—without extra work.

Automation in Google Sheets lets you act like a developer, without needing to be one.

2. What You Can Automate

Let's break it down with real examples. You can automate:

Task	Example
Email Reminders	Send alerts when a due date is near
Data Cleanup	Automatically remove rows marked "Done"
Custom Functions	Create your own reusable formulas
Form Handling	Move Google Form submissions to a custom layout
Reporting	Generate daily summaries or PDF reports
Data Import	Pull in live data from websites or external Sheets
Google Apps Integration	Create events in Calendar or send bulk emails from Gmail

Pro Tip:

Most automations in Sheets use a tool called Google Apps Script—a powerful coding platform that lives right inside your spreadsheet.

Automation isn't just about speed—it's about building smarter workflows that save time and reduce stress.

II. INTRODUCTION TO GOOGLE APPS SCRIPT

1. What Is Apps Script?

Google Apps Script is a JavaScript-based language created by Google to help you automate tasks across all Google products like Sheets, Docs, Gmail, Calendar, Drive, and more.

It lets you: Add custom buttons and menus; automatically send emails; move, format, or clean data; connect Sheets to external tools; trigger actions based on time or events.

Best part? It's already built into Google Sheets—no need to install anything.

2. Accessing the Script Editor

Let's get started with the Apps Script environment.

How to open the editor:

1. Open your Google Sheet.
2. Go to the menu: Extensions > Apps Script.
3. A new tab will open with the Script Editor.
4. You'll see a blank function named myFunction()—you can delete or replace it.

3. Your First Script: "Hello, Sheet!"

Let's write a tiny program that writes "Hello, Sheet!" in cell A1.

Type this in the editor:

```
function helloSheet() {
  SpreadsheetApp.getActiveSpreadsheet()
    .getActiveSheet()
    .getRange("A1")
    .setValue("Hello, Sheet!");
}
```

What it does:

- SpreadsheetApp gives access to your spreadsheet.
- .getActiveSpreadsheet() grabs the current sheet.
- .getRange("A1") selects cell A1.
- .setValue("Hello, Sheet!") writes text into that cell.

How to run:

1. Now click the ▶Run button at the top.
2. You may be asked to authorize the script (Google needs permission).
3. Then go back to your Sheet... and cell A1 says "Hello, Sheet!".

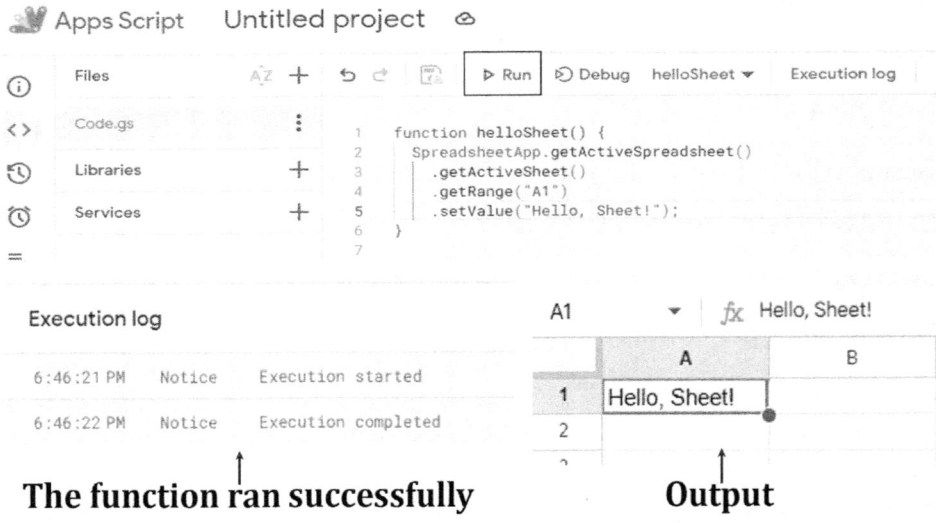

The function ran successfully   Output

III. AUTOMATING COMMON TASKS

In this section, you'll learn to build scripts that do your dirty work - like sending reminders, cleaning up old rows, and even moving data around automatically.

Note: Please remember to check our bonus to download all the scripts used in this chapter.

1. AUTO-SEND EMAIL REMINDERS

Let's say you have a sheet that tracks deadlines. You want to send an email when a task is due in 3 days.

Sample Sheet:

Task	Due Date	Status
Report Q1	4/19/2025	In Progress
Design Mock	4/07/2025	Not Started

Script: Send Alert if Due in 3 Days

```
function sendDueDateReminders() {
  const sheet = SpreadsheetApp.getActiveSpreadsheet().getActiveSheet();
  const data = sheet.getDataRange().getValues();
  const today = new Date();

  for (let i = 1; i < data.length; i++) {
    let task = data[i][0];
    let dueDate = new Date(data[i][1]);
    let status = data[i][2];

    let daysUntilDue = Math.ceil((dueDate - today) / (1000 * 60 * 60 * 24));

    if (daysUntilDue === 3 && status !== "Done") {
      MailApp.sendEmail(
        "your-email@example.com",    ←———— Your email
        "Reminder: " + task + " is due soon!",
        `The task "${task}" is due on ${dueDate.toDateString()}.`
      );
    }
  }
}
```

Customize:

- Change "your-email@example.com" to your own address.
- Adjust the days from 3 to anything you'd like.

2. AUTOMATICALLY CLEAR OR ARCHIVE DATA

Let's say you want to remove all rows where the task is marked "Done".

Task	Due Date	Status
Submit report	04/20/2025	In Progress
Design brochure	04/22/2025	Done
Prepare workshop	04/25/2025	Not Started
Create presentation slides	04/21/2025	Done
Call client	04/23/2025	In Progress

Script: Delete Rows Where Status = "Done":

```
function clearCompletedTasks() {
  const sheet = SpreadsheetApp.getActiveSheet();
  const data = sheet.getDataRange().getValues();

  for (let i = data.length - 1; i >= 1; i--) {
    if (data[i][2] === "Done") {
      sheet.deleteRow(i + 1); // +1 to account for header row
    }
  }
}
```

Always loop backwards when deleting rows to avoid skipping any!

3. TRIGGERING SCRIPTS AUTOMATICALLY

Want this to run daily without opening the sheet?

How to Add a Trigger:

1. Open Script Editor.
2. Click the clock icon in the left sidebar (Triggers).
3. Click + Add Trigger or Create a new trigger.
4. Choose:
   » Which function to run (e.g., sendDueDateReminders).
   » Select Event source: Time-driven.
   » Failure notification settings: Daily, or Every hour, etc.

IV. CREATING SIMPLE CUSTOM FUNCTIONS

1. WHY CREATE CUSTOM FUNCTIONS?

Sometimes, built-in formulas just don't cut it. You might need to: Add a special tax to values; convert hours to minutes; extract something oddly specific from a string; create a reusable calculation that's easier to understand.

That's where custom functions come in. They look and work just like regular functions: =ADDVAT(100). But you write the logic behind it yourself using Apps Script.

2. YOUR FIRST CUSTOM FUNCTION: ADD TAX

Let's create a function that adds 10% tax to any number.

Product	Base Price	Price with 10% VAT
T-Shirt	150	=ADDVAT(B2)
Jeans	320	=ADDVAT(B3)
Sneakers	500	=ADDVAT(B4)
Backpack	250	=ADDVAT(B5)
Cap	120	=ADDVAT(B6)

Script:

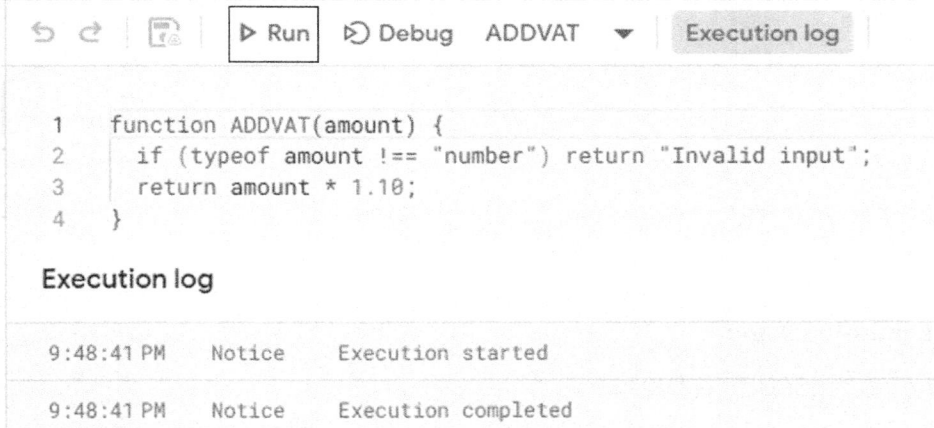

Use it in a Sheet like this:

=ADDVAT(200)

→ Returns 220.

How It Works:

Line	What It Does
function ADDVAT(amount)	Defines your custom function name and input
typeof amount !== "number"	Checks for bad input
return amount * 1.10;	Returns the taxed amount (adds 10%)

Naming Tip: Custom function names are not case-sensitive, but by convention, they're written in UPPERCASE (like built-in functions).

3. A Custom Function With Multiple Inputs

Product	Original Price	Discount Rate	Price After Discount
T-Shirt	100	0.2	=APPLYDISCOUNT(B2, C2)
Jeans	150	0.15	=APPLYDISCOUNT(B3, C3)
Sneakers	200	0.1	=APPLYDISCOUNT(B4, C4)
Backpack	120	0.25	=APPLYDISCOUNT(B5, C5)
Cap	50	0.1	=APPLYDISCOUNT(B6, C6)

Let's say you want to calculate a discount:

Example usage:

=APPLYDISCOUNT(100, 0.2)

→ Returns 80.

You can use this in any cell, and it'll recalculate when inputs change - just like =SUM().

Best Practices for Custom Functions:

Tip	Why It Matters
Always use return	Or else the cell will be blank
Add basic error checking	Prevents weird output like "undefined"
Comment your function logic	Helps you remember what it does later
Keep it short and reusable	One job per function is best

Pro Tip: Custom functions can't modify other cells, only return values to the cell they're written in.

Bonus: Add Help Text (for power users)

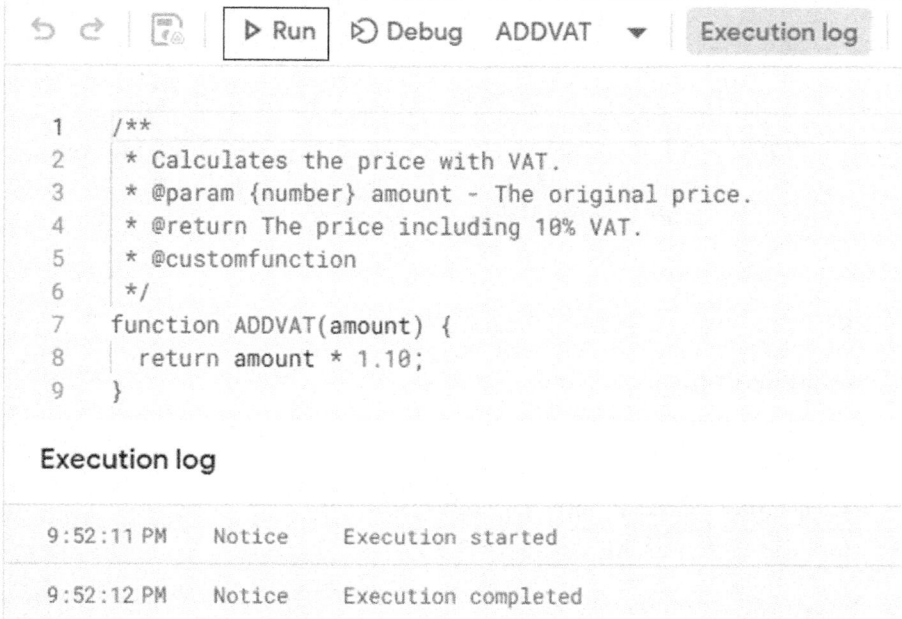

You can use JSDoc-style comments to show help hints.

This helps other users understand what the function does when they hover over it.

V. CONNECTING SHEETS WITH IMPORT FUNCTIONS

IMPORT functions are some of the most powerful tools in Google Sheets. They allow you to automatically pull in live data from: Other Google Sheets; CSV or TSV files; public websites (headlines, prices, links); external tools and feeds.

Let's break down the three major import functions: IMPORTDATA, IMPORTXML, and IMPORTRANGE.

1. IMPORTDATA – Pull CSV or TSV from a URL

Use this function to fetch raw data files hosted online, such as spreadsheets exported to .csv format.

Syntax:

=IMPORTDATA("https://example.com/data.csv")

Use Cases: Public GitHub CSV files; Google Drive files shared with "Anyone with the link"; exported reports from other apps/tools.

Tip: Make sure the link is direct to the file and not a download page.

2. IMPORTXML – SCRAPE WEBSITE DATA (ADVANCED!)

Want to pull live stock prices, news headlines, weather, or product names directly from a website? Use IMPORTXML, which uses XPath queries to extract content from structured HTML/XML pages.

Syntax:

=IMPORTXML("https://example.com", "//h2")

Real-World Examples:

- Headlines from a news site: =IMPORTXML("https://www.bbc.com", "//h2").
- Prices from product pages (Amazon, eBay, etc.).
- Meta descriptions, links, dates.

	A
1	US has stake in securing 'peaceful' future for Ukraine, White House says after resource deal
2	Seven takeaways from US-Ukraine resources deal
3	US has stake in securing 'peaceful' future for Ukraine, White House says after resource deal
4	Seven takeaways from US-Ukraine resources deal
5	Trump's national security adviser Mike Waltz leaves post, US media reports
6	We don't care': A defiant China looks beyond Trump's America
7	Watch: If you were Australia PM how would you handle the US and China?
8	Kamala Harris hits out at Trump in first major speech since losing election
9	Watch: Trump says US kids might have 'two dolls instead of 30' due to tariffs
10	Only from the BBC
11	The secrets of feeding the papal conclave
12	10 of the best TV shows to watch this May
13	Interview
14	Men are struggling. What does it mean for women?
15	More news

3. IMPORTRANGE – Connect to Other Google Sheets

This is a function for anyone managing data across multiple spreadsheets.

Syntax:

=IMPORTRANGE("spreadsheet_url", "Sheet1!A1:D10")

Example:

=IMPORTRANGE("https://docs.google.com/spreadsheets/d/abc123xyz", "SalesData!A1:C100")

What It Does:

- Pulls data from another Google Sheet and keeps it synced live.
- Works great for dashboards, consolidated reports, or multi-user workflows.

First-time use: You'll get a prompt to "Allow access" between the sheets. Click "Allow".

	A	B	C	D	J	K
1	Task	Due Date	Status			
2	Task 1	2025-05-01	In Progress			
3	Task 2	2025-06-01	Not Started			

URL

Pro Tips for Importing:

Tip	Why It Helps
Use named ranges when possible	Keeps your formulas readable
Keep imported ranges clean	Avoid merged cells and blank headers
Combine with QUERY() or FILTER()	Pull only the rows or columns you actually need
Avoid importing more than needed	Helps performance and readability

Bonus: Combine IMPORTRANGE + QUERY

Want to pull only filtered data from another sheet?

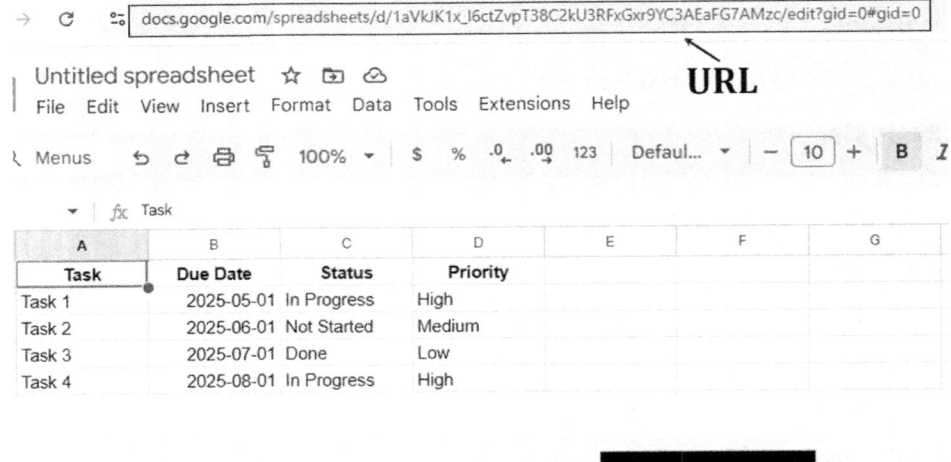

Formula

VI. GOOGLE FORMS + SHEETS INTEGRATION

1. CREATING A FORM CONNECTED TO A SHEET

Google Forms is one of the easiest ways to collect data—and when connected to Sheets, your submissions become a live, organized database you can automate.

How to Create and Link a Form:

1. In Google Drive, click New > Google Form.
2. Design your form (e.g., Name, Email, Feedback).

3. Click Responses tab > Link to Sheets.

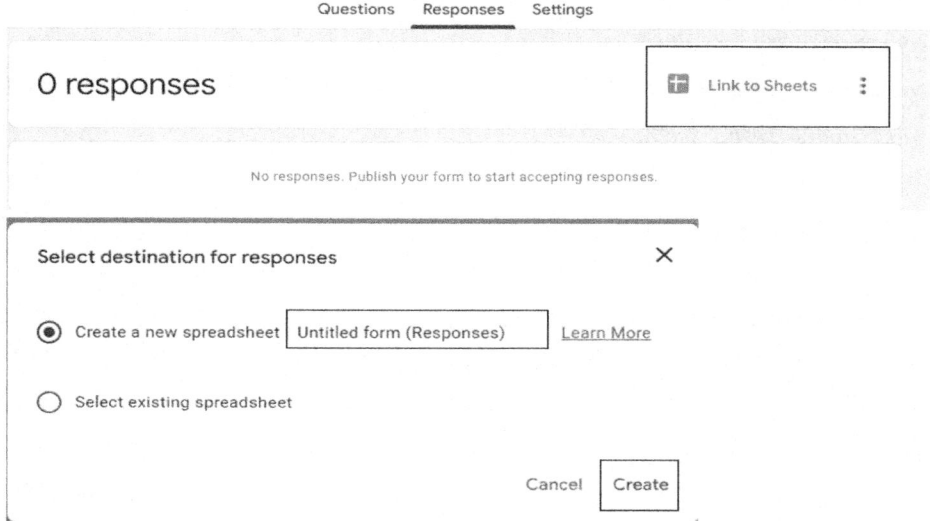

4. Choose "Create new spreadsheet" or link to an existing one.
5. Boom! Every submission gets logged to a Sheet in real-time.

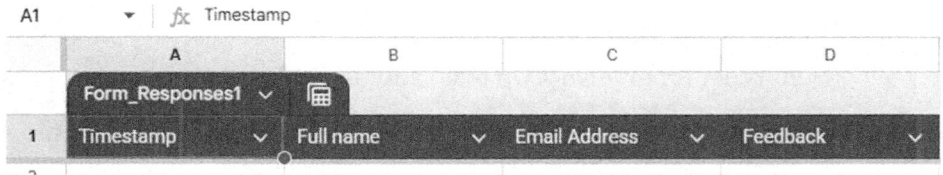

2. SHEET VIEW AFTER LINKING

Once connected, your Sheet will look like this:

Timestamp	Name	Email	Feedback
4/6/25 10:01 AM	Jenny	jenny@email.com	Loved it!
4/6/25 10:03 AM	Mark	mark@email.com	Needs improvement

You can now use this as a trigger for automations, a data source for dashboards, or a record for reporting.

3. AUTOMATING FORM RESPONSES

Let's say you want to send a thank-you email each time someone submits feedback.

Script: Auto-Send Response Email

```
function sendAutoReply(e) {
  const responses = e.values;
  const name = responses[1];
  const email = responses[2];

  MailApp.sendEmail({
    to: email,
    subject: "Thanks for your feedback!",
    body: `Hi ${name},\n\nThanks for your response. We appreciate your input!\n\n-The Team`
  });
}
```

To Set This Up:

1. In the script editor, go to Triggers > Add Trigger.
2. Choose:
   » Function: sendAutoReply.
   » Event type: From form > On form submit.

More Use Cases for Forms + Sheets:

Use Case	Automation Idea
Job applications	Auto-filter by role or experience
Event RSVPs	Send calendar invites automatically
Feedback/Surveys	Analyze results and create live charts
Contact forms	Send email alerts to team, log leads in CRM

Pro Tips:

- Always test your form + script setup before going live.
- Use e.values to access form data in order of questions.
- You can add confirmation logic (e.g., check for duplicates).

VII. CONNECTING TO OTHER GOOGLE SERVICES

Google Sheets is more than just a data tool - it's a launchpad for interacting with the entire Google Workspace. In this section, you'll learn how to Send personalized emails via Gmail; add events to Google Calendar; create and organize files in Google Drive.

1. CONNECTING TO GMAIL

Want to send bulk emails from a Sheet—like a client update or a thank-you message?

Script: Send Personalized Emails

	A	B	C
1	**Name**	**Email**	**Status**
2	Jonathan Smith	████@gmail.com	Sent
3	Evan Brown	████@gmail.com	Sent
4	Katie Miller	████@email.com	Sent

```
function sendEmailsFromSheet() {
  const sheet = SpreadsheetApp.getActiveSpreadsheet().getActiveSheet();
  const data = sheet.getDataRange().getValues();
  for (let i = 1; i < data.length; i++) {
    const name = data[i][0];
    const email = data[i][1];
    const status = data[i][2];
    if (status !== "Sent") {
      const subject = "Thanks for your submission!";
      const body = `Hi ${name},\n\nWe've received your info. Thanks!\n\n- The Team`;
      MailApp.sendEmail(email, subject, body);
      // Mark as Sent
      sheet.getRange(i + 1, 3).setValue("Sent");
    }
  }
}
```

2. CONNECTING TO GOOGLE CALENDAR

Want to turn your Sheet into an event planner? You can auto-create Calendar events from a table of tasks or meetings.

Script: Create Calendar Events from Sheet

	A	B	C	D
1	Date	Event Title	Description	
2	4/20/2025	Team Meeting	Discuss project progress	
3	4/21/2025	Client Call	Call with ABC Corporation	
4	4/22/2025	Product Demo	Demo for new clients	

```
function addCalendarEvents() {
  const sheet = SpreadsheetApp.getActiveSpreadsheet().getActiveSheet();
  const data = sheet.getRange("A2:C").getValues(); // Date, Title, Description
  const calendar = CalendarApp.getDefaultCalendar();

  for (let i = 0; i < data.length; i++) {
    const date = new Date(data[i][0]);
    const title = data[i][1];
    const desc = data[i][2];

    if (title && date) {
      calendar.createAllDayEvent(title, date, { description: desc });
    }
  }
}
```

Use Case: Event reminders, class schedules, interview slots, etc.

3. CONNECTING TO GOOGLE DRIVE

You can even automatically create and organize files - like invoices, certificates, or reports - from data in your sheet.

Script: Export Sheet as PDF to Drive

```
function exportSheetToDrivePDF() {
  const spreadsheet = SpreadsheetApp.getActiveSpreadsheet();
  const sheet = spreadsheet.getActiveSheet();

const url = 'https://docs.google.com/spreadsheets/d/${spreadsheet.getID()}/mat=pdf&portrait=true&sheetnames=false&printtitle=false&pagenumber=false&gridlines=false&fzr=false&gird=${sheet.getSheetID()}';
  const token = ScriptApp.getOAuthToken();
  const response = UrlFetchApp.fetch(url, {
    headers: {
      Authorization: `Bearer ${token}`,
    },
  });
DriveApp.createFile(response.getBlob()).setName(`${sheet.getName()} Report.pdf`);
}
```

What it does:

Exports the current sheet as a PDF and saves it to your Google Drive—automatically.

VIII. BEST PRACTICES FOR SHEET AUTOMATION

Automation is powerful—but it also needs to be handled with care. A small error in your script could delete rows, send the wrong email, or overwrite data unintentionally.

This section gives you proven tips for writing reliable, maintainable, and safe automation scripts.

1. TEST EVERYTHING IN A COPY FIRST

Never test scripts on your main file:

- Always work on a duplicate or sandbox version of your sheet.
- Try your scripts with dummy data first.
- Simulate your full workflow end-to-end.

HOW TO MAKE A TEST COPY:

- File > Make a copy → Rename as "Test Sheet".

2. KEEP SCRIPTS MODULAR AND DOCUMENTED

Writing one massive function = headache later.

Instead: Break your automation into small functions, each with a single purpose.

- Add comments like this:

```
// This function sends a reminder if task is due in 3 days
function sendReminder(taskName, dueDate, email) {
  // logic here
}
```

Benefits: Easier to troubleshoot; easier for others (or future-you) to understand; easier to reuse in other projects.

3. HANDLE ERRORS GRACEFULLY

Use try/catch for Apps Script:

```
function sendEmails() {
  const sheet = SpreadsheetApp.getActiveSpreadsheet().getActiveSheet();
  const data = sheet.getDataRange().getValues(); // Get data from the sheet
  for (let i = 1; i < data.length; i++) {
    const name = data[i][0]; // Recipient's name
    const email = data[i][1]; // Recipient's email
    const subject = "Congratulations!";
    const body = `Hi ${name},\n\nThank you for your participation!`;
    try {
      // Try sending the email
      MailApp.sendEmail(email, subject, body);
      Logger.log("Successfully sent email to: " + email);
    } catch (e) {
      // If an error occurs, log the error message
      Logger.log("Error sending email to " + email + ": " + e.message);
    }
  }
}
```

Use IFERROR() in formulas:

`=IFERROR(VLOOKUP(A2, Products!A:B, 2, FALSE), "Not found")`

This keeps your sheet from looking broken with #N/A or #REF! everywhere.

Summary: Top 5 Automation Best Practices:

Best Practice	Why It Matters
Test in a copy	Prevents real data loss
Break code into small functions	Easier to debug and reuse
Comment your scripts	Improves readability and collaboration
Use error handling	Avoids crashes and broken workflows
Name your triggers clearly	Helps track what runs when

Bonus: Use Logs for Debugging

Use Logger.log() to track what your code is doing:

```
function sendReminder(email) {
  Logger.log("Sending reminder to: " + email);
  MailApp.sendEmail(email, "Reminder", "Don't forget your appointment!");
}
```

Then view it in:

View > Logs

Pro Tip: Script Naming

Give your functions names that are:

- Descriptive: sendInvoiceReminder().
- Verb-based: archiveCompletedTasks().
- Consistent: processX, createY, updateZ.

IX. MINI AUTOMATION PROJECTS

Each of these automation workflows is designed to be: Simple to set up; useful for business or personal tasks; a launchpad for your own creative automations.

1. Project 1: Daily Sales Summary Email

Goal: Send an automatic email with today's total sales.

Setup: Your sheet includes:

Date	Product	Amount
4/6/2025	Widget A	$40
4/6/2025	Widget B	$60

Script:

```
function sendDailySalesSummary() {
  const sheet = SpreadsheetApp.getActiveSheet();
  const data = sheet.getDataRange().getValues();
  const today = Utilities.formatDate(new Date(), Session.getScriptTimeZone(), "MM/dd/yyyy");
  let total = 0;
  for (let i = 1; i < data.length; i++) {
    let date = Utilities.formatDate(new Date(data[i][0]), Session.getScriptTimeZone(), "MM/dd/yyyy");
    if (date === today) {
      total += parseFloat(data[i][2]);
    }
  }
  MailApp.sendEmail("your@email.com", " Today's Sales Summary", `Total Sales for ${today}: $${total}`);
}
```

Note: Add a time-driven trigger to run every morning.

2. Project 2: Inventory Reorder Alert

Goal: Notify when an item falls below its minimum stock level.

Setup:

Item	Quantity	Min Level
Pens	12	10
Notebooks	4	5

SCRIPT:

```
function sendInventoryAlert() {
  const sheet = SpreadsheetApp.getActiveSheet();
  const data = sheet.getRange("A2:C").getValues();
  let message = "";
  for (let i = 0; i < data.length; i++) {
    const item = data[i][0];
    const qty = Number(data[i][1]);
    const min = Number(data[i][2]);
    if (qty < min) {
      message += `${item} is low: Only ${qty} left (min required: ${min})\n`;
    }
  }
  if (message !== "") {
    MailApp.sendEmail("email@company.com", "Restock Alert", message);
  }
}
```

3. PROJECT 3: AUTO-COPY FORM SUBMISSIONS TO MASTER SHEET

Goal: Collect responses from multiple Google Forms into a central master sheet.

STEPS:

1. Each form is linked to its own Sheet (e.g., Form1, Form2).
2. Master Sheet will pull responses using IMPORTRANGE.

FORMULA EXAMPLE (IN MASTER SHEET):

```
=QUERY(
  {IMPORTRANGE("URL1", "Form Responses 1!A2:C"),
  IMPORTRANGE("URL2", "Form Responses 1!A2:C")},
  "SELECT Col1, Col2, Col3 WHERE Col2 IS NOT NULL", 0)
```

This creates a live, centralized database from multiple forms.

Chapter 8: Productivity Tips, Shortcuts & Advanced Troubleshooting

This chapter gives you the power user edge: Save time with keyboard shortcuts; use Google's hidden tools to get more done; collaborate like a pro; solve frustrating errors fast; optimize performance in even the most complex sheets.

Let's go section by section, starting with shortcuts.

I. KEYBOARD SHORTCUTS THAT SPEED EVERYTHING UP

1. Why Use Shortcuts?

If you use Sheets daily - even weekly - shortcuts are the #1 way to double your speed.

You'll: Jump across large data sets; format cells faster; enter and clean data efficiently; look like a spreadsheet wizard.

2. Must-Know Shortcuts (Windows/Mac)

Navigation:

Action	Shortcut (Windows)	Shortcut (Mac)
Jump to end of data	Ctrl + Arrow	Cmd + Arrow
Go to top-left (A1)	Ctrl + Home	Cmd + ↑
Go to bottom-right	Ctrl + End	Cmd + ↓

Formatting:

Action	Shortcut (Windows)	Shortcut (Mac)
Bold / Italic / Underline	Ctrl + B / I / U	Cmd + B / I / U
Format as number	Ctrl + Shift + 1	⌘ + Shift + 1
Format as currency	Ctrl + Shift + 4	⌘ + Shift + 4

Editing & Input:

Action	Shortcut (Windows)	Shortcut (Mac)
Fill down	Ctrl + D	Cmd + D

Action	Shortcut (Windows)	Shortcut (Mac)
Undo / Redo	Ctrl + Z / Y	Cmd + Z / Shift + Z
Insert current date	Ctrl + ;	Cmd + Shift + ;
Select entire row	Shift + Space	Same
Select entire column	Ctrl + Space	Cmd + Space

3. Full Shortcut Reference

Want to see all shortcuts available?

- Press Ctrl + / (Windows) or Cmd + / (Mac).
- Google Sheets will show a pop-up of every available shortcut, categorized by function.

Pro Tips:

- Create your own "hotkey list" of 5 favorites to memorize.
- Practice 1-2 new shortcuts per week for muscle memory.
- Combine with autofill and formula tips for maximum speed.
- Press Enter or click the checkmark to accept.

II. COLLABORATION TIPS FOR TEAMS

1. Commenting & Suggesting

Collaboration isn't just about editing—it's about communicating inside the sheet.

Add a Comment:

- Right-click a cell → Click "Comment".
- OR use the shortcut: Ctrl + Alt + M (Cmd + Option + M on Mac).

Tag a Teammate:

- Use @email or @name to tag teammates.
- They'll get an email notification.

Use Comments For:

- Questions on data entries.
- Flagging cells that need updates.

- Assigning follow-up tasks.

2. SHEET PROTECTION & CELL LOCKING

Prevent teammates from accidentally editing formulas or sensitive data.

Protect a Range or Sheet:

- Choose a range (e.g., totals, headers, dashboards).
- Set who can edit it (only you, or specific collaborators).

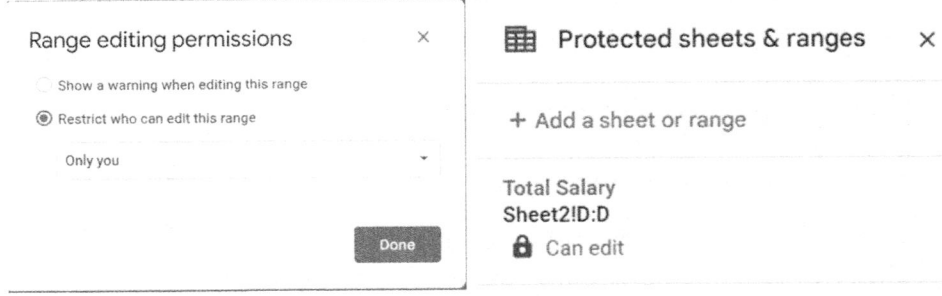

Best Practices for Team Collaboration:

Tip	Why It Helps
Use comments instead of edits	Keeps communication organized
Share as "Commenter" when unsure	Avoids accidental changes
Protect critical cells/ranges	Keeps formulas and layout intact
Use version history	Roll back if someone makes a big mistake
Train teammates on sheet etiquette	Prevents confusion and chaos

III. OPTIMIZING PERFORMANCE IN LARGE SHEETS

1. Common Slowdown Issues

Even though Google Sheets is powerful, it has limits. The biggest performance killers are:

Problem	Cause
Slow loading or freezing	Too many formulas or large data sets
Lag when editing	Volatile functions recalculating constantly (e.g., NOW(), RAND())
Delayed response in dashboards	Complex ARRAYFORMULA, QUERY, IMPORTRANGE combos
Slow opening time	Heavy formatting and linked files

2. Tips for Improving Speed

- Use Open-Ended Ranges Sparingly:
  » Avoid formulas like =SUM(A:A) on large columns.
  » Instead: =SUM(A2:A1000) or use Named Ranges.
- Replace Volatile Functions:
  » Functions like NOW(), TODAY(), RAND(), and RANDBETWEEN() recalculate every time the sheet is touched.
  » Replace them with static values if updates aren't needed every second.
- Limit ARRAYFORMULA:
  » Only use it when necessary. Avoid stacking ARRAYFORMULA on top of other heavy functions like VLOOKUP or IMPORTRANGE.

3. Use Cleanup Tools

Google Sheets offers built-in help: Data > Data Cleanup. You can:

- Remove duplicate rows.
- Trim whitespace.
- Standardize formatting.

This reduces unnecessary background processing and helps formulas run faster.

4. EXTRA TIPS FOR LARGE FILES

Strategy	Why It Helps
Use multiple tabs	Break up huge datasets
Use helper columns	Avoid long, nested formulas
Avoid conditional formatting over blank rows	It slows down the entire sheet
Limit linked sheets	IMPORTRANGE() is powerful but resource-heavy
Set Calculation to "On change and every minute"	Ensures your sheet updates time-based formulas automatically

To change calculation settings: File > Settings > Calculation tab.

IV. PRO-LEVEL TIPS & HIDDEN FEATURES

1. CREATE CUSTOM MENUS WITH APPS SCRIPT

You can add your own buttons and menu items to Google Sheets using a few lines of Google Apps Script.

Example: Add a Custom Menu

- This creates a new menu called "My Tools".
- Adds two actions: one to send a report, one to clear the sheet.

2. USE ADD-ONS TO EXTEND GOOGLE SHEETS

Google Sheets has a whole ecosystem of add-ons you can plug in for advanced features.

Popular Add-Ons:

```
function onOpen() {
  const ui = SpreadsheetApp.getUi();
  ui.createMenu('My Tools')
    .addItem('Send Weekly Report', 'sendWeeklyReport')
    .addSeparator()
    .addItem('Clear Sheet', 'clearSheet')
    .addToUi();
}
```

Add-On	What It Does
Supermetrics	Pull marketing data from platforms like Facebook, Google Ads
Autocrat	Merge data into Docs or PDFs, and auto-email them
Power Tools	All-in-one toolkit for cleaning, merging, formatting
Sheetgo	Automate data transfers across spreadsheets

To browse add-ons: Extensions > Add-ons > Get Add-ons.

3. NAMED RANGES FOR FAST NAVIGATION

If your sheet has many tabs or massive datasets, named ranges help you stay organized and work faster.

How to Name a Range:

- Select a cell or range → Right-click → "Define named range".
- Instead of using A2:A100, you can now write: =SUM(MyExpenses).
- Named ranges are easier to read and maintain in long formulas.

Tips Recap:

Power Tip	Why You'll Love It
Custom menus	Add your own tools directly in the toolbar
Add-ons	Unlock automation, analytics, PDF tools, etc.
Named ranges	Make formulas cleaner and easier to update
Shortcuts + Smart Fill	Supercharge your data entry
Script buttons (bonus)	Trigger actions with a single click

V. END-OF-CHAPTER CHECKLIST

Use this checklist to review and reinforce your skills:

Keyboard Mastery:

☐ Know at least 5 keyboard shortcuts that save me time.

☐ Can jump to the bottom of data or fill down formulas with ease.

☐ Can open the full shortcut menu with Ctrl + / (or Cmd + /).

Smart Tools:

☐ Used the Explore tool to get quick insights or charts.

☐ Tested Smart Fill to complete patterns automatically.

Safety & Recovery:

☐ Know how to use Version History to undo mistakes.

☐ Named key versions for major template updates.

Collaboration Superpowers:

☐ Can comment and tag teammates directly in cells.

☐ Shared sheets with proper permission levels (Viewer, Commenter, Editor).

☐ Used Protected Ranges to safeguard formulas or layouts.

Formula Fixing:

☐ Recognize and understand common errors like #REF!, #DIV/0!, and #N/A.

☐ Can debug formulas by breaking them down.

☐ Use IFERROR() to keep sheets clean and user-friendly.

Performance Tuning:

☐ Know how to reduce lag by limiting volatile functions.

☐ Used Cleanup suggestions to simplify messy data.

☐ Set sheets to recalculate only when needed.

Pro-Level Features:

☐ Tried a custom menu using Google Apps Script.

☐ Explored powerful Add-ons like Autocrat or Power Tools.

☐ Defined and used Named Ranges in formulas.

If you checked most of these off—you're officially a Google Sheets Power User! You've gone from beginner to expert, built real-world projects, automated tasks, and learned to troubleshoot like a pro.

Conclusion & Bonuses

I. GOOGLE SHEETS MASTERY: FROM BEGINNER TO EXPERT IN ONE BOOK

Congratulations! You've just completed a deep dive into the world of Google Sheets—from navigating the basics to building dashboards, automating workflows, and troubleshooting like a spreadsheet ninja.

You didn't just learn what to do—you learned how to think in Google Sheets. That's true mastery.

1. What You've Accomplished

- Built your first smart spreadsheets.
- Mastered essential and advanced formulas.
- Created visual dashboards to tell data stories.
- Automated tasks to save hours of work.
- Built real-world tools like CRMs, budget trackers, and invoice generators.
- Debugged errors and optimized performance like a power user.

II. KEEP THE MOMENTUM GOING

1. Practice with Real Data

Use your own budget, project tracker, or business info to reinforce what you've learned.

2. Explore Google Workspace Integration

Experiment with Google Forms, Docs, Calendar, and Gmail. Sheets becomes 10x more powerful when it's connected to the tools you use every day.

3. Join Communities

Ask questions and discover new tricks:

- Reddit: r/googlesheets.
- Google Docs Editors Help Community.
- YouTube creators like Learn Google Spreadsheets and Leila Gharani.

4. **Looking Ahead**

Want to go even further?

- Master Google Apps Script with full automation tutorials.
- Learn how to build custom business tools using Sheets as a database.
- Use Google Data Studio (now Looker Studio) for next-level visual reporting.
- Try out integrations with Zapier, Make (Integromat), or AppSheet for no-code apps.

The best spreadsheet isn't the one with the fanciest formulas or the flashiest charts—it's the one that solves a real problem. Keep building, keep solving, and keep learning.

Thanks for reading, and remember: Data is only as powerful as your ability to use it.

See you in your next spreadsheet adventure!

5. **Bonuses**

I have prepared two special bonus resources you can download and use alongside the lessons:

1. Sample Scripts Collection: A ready-to-use set of Google Apps Script examples to help you automate repetitive tasks, send emails directly from Sheets, and supercharge your productivity.
2. Cheat Sheet: Most-Used Formulas & Shortcuts - A quick reference guide for the formulas and keyboard shortcuts you'll use most often, designed to save you time and keep you focused.

Don't forget to scan the QR code below (or click on the link if you are reading the ebook) to access the bonuses.

Link

Thank You

Before we say goodbye, I want to say a heartfelt thank you for choosing this book.

Whether you're a student trying to stay on top of assignments, a freelancer managing client projects, or a small business owner looking for a smarter way to organize your data—this book was written with you in mind

I know that spreadsheets can feel intimidating at first. Maybe you've opened Google Sheets before but never felt fully confident with formulas, or perhaps you've relied on Excel for years and wondered if Sheets could really replace it. That's exactly why I created this guide: to make Google Sheets approachable, practical, and powerful—even if you've never used a spreadsheet program seriously before.

Share the Love

If this book helped you unlock the power of Google Sheets, saved you hours of frustration, or simply made things "click," would you consider leaving a short review?

It takes less than a minute, costs nothing, and it means the world to authors like me. Honest reviews help more readers discover this guide, and they motivate me to continue creating useful, real-world resources.

Scan the QR code below to leave a review or tap the link (if you're reading the ebook).

Link

Explore More

If you enjoyed this book, I invite you to explore more titles in my productivity series—covering tools like Excel, Word, QuickBooks, and Office 365. Each book is designed to be straightforward, hands-on, and packed with examples to help you grow your skills and work smarter.

Scan the QR code below to see the full series.

Something Not Quite Right?

If you run into issues, notice something missing, or have ideas for improving the next edition, I'd love to hear from you.

Please reach out anytime at ethanwellsreads@gmail.com. I genuinely want this book to be as helpful as possible, and your feedback makes all the difference.

Thanks again for trusting me as your guide. I'm wishing you every success as you master Google Sheets—one sheet, one formula, one smart workflow at a time.

With gratitude,

Ethan Wells

Printed in Dunstable, United Kingdom